THE WAY
TO WEALTH

Part 1
The Journey Begins

Success Strategies of
the Wealthy Entrepreneur

THE WAY TO WEALTH

Part 1
The Journey Begins

Success Strategies of
the Wealthy Entrepreneur

BRIAN TRACY

Ep Entrepreneur® Press

Editorial Director: Jere Calmes
Cover Design: Beth Hansen-Winter
Production and Editorial Services: CWL Publishing Enterprises, Inc.,
Madison, Wisconsin, www.cwlpub.com

This publication is designed to provide accurate and authoritative
information in regard to the subject matter covered. It is sold with the
understanding that the publisher is not engaged in rendering legal,
accounting, or other professional services. If legal advice or other
expert assistance is required, the services of a competent professional
person should be sought.
—From a Declaration of Principles jointly adopted by a
Committee of the American Bar Association and
a Committee of Publishers and Associations

ISBN 1-59918-050-2

Library of Congress Cataloging-in-Publication Data
Tracy, Brian.
  The way to wealth part 1 the journey begins : success strategies of
  the wealthy entrepreneur / by Brian Tracy.
    p. cm.
  Includes index.
  ISBN 1-59918-050-2 (alk. paper)
  1. Entrepreneurship. 2. Entrepreneurship—Psychological aspects.
  3. New business enterprises—Management. 4. Success in business.
  I. Title.
  HB615.T73 2007
  658.4'21--dc22

                                    2006023723

Printed in Canada

11 10 09 08 07 06   10 9 8 7 6 5 3 2 1

DEDICATION

This book is lovingly dedicated to my children and their partners, Christina and Damon, Michael and Tasha, David and Sara, and Catherine. You are the entrepreneurs and business builders of the future and the focal points of all my hopes and aspirations for success and happiness.

CONTENTS

Contents

Contents

Contents

Contents

Welcome to the Golden Age

> In America, every day is a new beginning, and every sunset is merely the latest milestone on a voyage that never ends. For this is the land that has never become, but is always in the act of becoming.
>
> —Ronald Reagan

elcome to the Golden Age of Humanity! This is the best time in all of human history to be alive, and it is only going to get better in the years ahead.

More people are starting more businesses and becoming wealthy in more ways than has ever been imaginable in all of human history. There are more opportunities and possibilities for you to achieve success, financial independence, and personal wealth than ever before. You just have to find out the right business for you personally and then to put your whole heart into realizing your full financial potential.

In 1900, after 200 years of growth and development in America, there were 5,000 millionaires, most of them self-made. That is to say, they started with nothing, often as penniless immigrants, and through hard work and sheer determination became wealthy.

By 2000, there were 5 million millionaires in America, an increase of 1,000 times! The technological and Internet boom of the 1990s played a major part in increasing the number of millionaires so dramatically. Then, after leveling off in 2001-2002, the number of millionaires jumped by 60 percent, to more than 8.3 million millionaires by 2006.

Just as in the past, fully 80 percent of these new millionaires, multimillionaires, and billionaires were self-made. They started with nothing and made all of their money in one generation. They were entrepreneurs, people who started their own businesses and made them successful by doing the things you will learn about in this book.

The Age of Entrepreneurship

According to the Organisation for Economic Development and Co-operation in Paris, the United States is now the most entrepreneurial country in the world. Fully 12 percent of Americans are working in businesses created in the last 42 months. 70 percent of all new jobs are being created by small and mid-sized companies, many of them start-ups. More opportunities are opening up for more people as entrepreneurs than ever before. Two million businesses are started each year.

Why is this happening? There are perhaps three key factors.

The first is the incredible explosion and expansion of information and ideas of all kinds. It is estimated that total knowledge doubles every two to three years. Almost 500,000 new books and millions of articles are published each year, on every conceivable subject.

Technology is expanding at an incredible rate as well. New products are pouring into the market each day, produced all over the world, each with a shelf life of no more than six months before it is made obsolete by another product.

Finally, competition is more aggressive than ever before. Competitors, both nationally and internationally, determined to achieve sales, success, and profitability, are combining new information and technology into new products and services at a breathtaking rate.

Today, all three factors—information, technology, and competition—are working together to accelerate the speed of change beyond anything that we have ever imagined. And, if anything, the speed of change and the number of opportunities and possibilities are going to increase and become greater in the months and years ahead.

The Entrepreneur as Sparkplug

The critical insight of modern economics, dating back to the Austrian School of the 1870s, is that the entrepreneur is the sparkplug in the engine of economic activity.

The entrepreneur is the person who has the special ability to turn an opportunity into profit by assembling resources—finance, labor, technology, facilities, machinery, and information—to produce products and services at a cost substantially below the price for which they can be sold in a competitive market.

The entrepreneur has the ability to identify a customer need and then satisfy that need cost-effectively, over and over, creating jobs, sales, profits, and revenues that had not existed before.

The British mega-entrepreneur Richard Branson once said, "Once you start and build a successful business, you can do it over and over; the principles remain the same."

Three Keys to Business Success

There are only three keys to starting and building a successful business, achieving personal prosperity, and becoming wealthy.

Step one is to find a product or service that people want and need and are willing to pay for at a price that enables you to make a profit.

Step two is to aggressively market and sell the product or service in sufficient quantity that you earn enough profit to be able to repeat the process over and over.

Step three is to learn how to manage, administer, and account for your income and expenses.

In more than 90 percent of businesses that have problems, there is a problem or weakness in one or more of these three areas.

In fact, it is estimated that fully 86 percent of businesses today are operating below their potential for sales and profitability because of a weakness in selecting the right product or service, selling it aggressively, or accounting and managing. If you are already in business, give yourself a grade of 1–10 in each of these areas. You will see immediately where you need to focus your efforts.

Just Over Broke

Most entrepreneurs have not really started a business. Instead, they have created a job (which means "just **over broke**") where they work harder, for longer hours, and earn less than they would working for someone else.

The tragedy is that the underachievement and frustration that most entrepreneurs experience is unnecessary. Starting and building a profitable business has been done millions of times by people with no business experience at all. And whatever hundreds of thousands and millions of other people have done throughout America and all over the world, you can do as well, if you simply learn how.

You Can Learn to Be Successful

Some years ago, I recognized a vacuum in entrepreneurial training. As a result, I assembled all of my years of experience, plus several hundred hours of research, into a program entitled *How You Can Start, Build, Manage or Turn Around Any Business*. I began to offer this program as a two-day seminar for entrepreneurs and business people of all kinds.

The results were extraordinary and immediate. Sometimes, in as little as a week, businesses that had been on the verge of collapse turned around completely. These entrepreneurs and business owners, now equipped with the essential skills of product development, marketing, sales, raising capital, and management, quickly turned losses into profits and began moving from frustration and failure to success and affluence.

The biggest producers of audio learning programs in the world, Nightingale-Conant Corporation of Chicago, produced this program as *How to Start and Succeed in Your Own Business* and turned it into a best seller. *Reader's Digest* concluded that *How to Start and Succeed in Your Own Business* was one of the top three educational audio learning programs produced in America in the 20th century—out of more than 800 reviewed.

The Way to Wealth is the "graduate program" on business building and entrepreneurship. This book contains the most practical, proven methods and techniques ever discovered for rapid, predictable increases in sales, revenues, and profitability.

There Are No Limits

The good news is that all business skills are *learnable*. All sales skills are learnable. All moneymaking skills of all kinds are learnable as well. You can learn any skill that you need to learn to achieve any goal that you can set for yourself. There are virtually no limits.

You may not be able to dunk basketballs like Michael Jordan or play classical violin like Igor Stravinsky, but you can learn any business or moneymaking skill. Every person who is excellent at making money in his or her own business today was once poor at making money and made a lot of mistakes. Everyone at the top was once at the bottom. Everyone who is at the front of the line of life started at the back of the line. And what others have done, you can do as well.

Once you master the skills of business building, which this book will help you to do far faster than you ever could on your own, you can use these skills over and over again. Each time you use a new business skill, you will get better at that skill. And as you get better and better, using these skills over and over, it will take you less and less time to achieve the same or greater financial results.

You have heard of "serial entrepreneurs." These are men and women who start and build business after business, making each one of them successful and profitable, putting them under good management or selling them, and moving on to the next business. Richard Branson is a perfect example.

What do these people have in common? It is simple. They have mastered the essential business skills necessary to select the right product or service, market and sell it in sufficient quantities to make it profitable, and then accurately account for income and expenses and manage the process.

Start with the Sale of Personal Services

Most fortunes in America, and throughout the world, start with the sale of personal services. Most people start off broke or with very little money. Most people have to learn all of their money-making skills from the very beginning. The top ten richest multi-billionaires in America in 2006, according to *Forbes* magazine, are: Bill Gates, Warren Buffett, Paul Allen, Michael Dell, Larry Ellison, and the five descendants of the family of Sam Walton, founder of Wal-Mart. They are all first-generation billionaires.

Of the more than 800 billionaires worldwide, most are first generation as well. Most millionaires, multimillionaires and centimillionaires start with nothing as well. What's your excuse?

Four Goals We All Share

We all start out with four primary goals in life. The first is to be healthy, enjoy high energy, and live a long life. Second, everyone wants to have good relationships with people they love and care about and who love and care about them. Third, everyone wants to do work that they find interesting and challenging and that pays very well. And the fourth common goal of humanity is to achieve financial independence, to reach the point where you have enough money so that you never have to worry about money again.

The best news is that it is more possible for you to achieve these four goals, at a higher level, faster, by starting and building your own successful business than in virtually any other way.

When you start and build your own successful business, you take complete control of your life. You become the master of your own destiny. You remove all limits to what you can do, have, and be in life. By building a successful business, you open up a world of opportunities and possibilities that the majority of people can only dream about.

As an entrepreneur and business builder, *The Way to Wealth* will show you how to achieve all your business goals faster and easier than you ever dreamed possible. Let's get started.

CHAPTER ONE

The Psychology of Entrepreneurship

To achieve something you have never achieved before, you have to become someone you have never been before; you must learn things that you have never known before.

—Les Brown

THERE IS A PSYCHOLOGICAL PRINCIPLE THAT SAYS, "YOU strive for those things as an adult that you felt that you were most deprived of as a child."

Well, I was deprived of most things. My parents were critical, cold, and unsupportive. As a result, I "acted out" in school and got into nothing but trouble. I was suspended and expelled multiple times and attended several schools throughout my young life. I was unpopular and had few friends. I got in trouble with the law as a teenager. I was voted "least likely to succeed." When I went back to visit my high school teachers as a 19-year-old, the first question they asked me was "Where have you been serving time?"

I left high school without graduating and worked at laboring jobs for several years. I started off as a dishwasher in the back of a small hotel. When I lost that job, I went on to washing cars in a car lot. Then, when I lost that job, I washed floors with a janitorial service. I thought washing was in my future, but it was a downhill trend.

And, by the way, "lost" when you are young is a euphemism for "involuntary career redeployment" (getting fired!). I worked in factories and sawmills. I worked in the brush with a chain saw and on farms and ranches. I worked as a construction laborer, carrying heavy construction materials from place to place. I dug ditches. One summer I dug wells for two months.

Starting with Nothing

I never had any money. I lived in my car in the wintertime and slept next to it in the summertime. I collected unemployment insurance and welfare. When I was 23 years old, I was an itinerant farm laborer, sleeping on the hay in the farmer's barn, eating with the farmer's family, and getting up in the dark. We had to be in the fields ready to work at dawn so that we could get the crop in before the first frost.

I was uneducated, unskilled, and, at the end of the harvest, once more unemployed. At that point, the only job that I could find was straight commission sales, cold calling from office to office during the day and from door to door on houses and apartments in the evenings.

I wasn't afraid of hard work; at least selling was clean work. They told me that, the more I got rejected, the more sales I would eventually make. I therefore ran from place to place so I could be rejected more often. One month I made more than 500 calls and not a single sale. I was just hanging on by my fingernails, occasionally making a small sale that enabled me to keep going a little while longer.

Learn from the Experts

Then one day, I did something that changed my life. I went to the most successful salesman in our company, a guy who was making ten times as much as anyone else in the office and working far less, and I asked him, "What are you doing differently from me?"

To my surprise, he stopped what he was doing and told me what he did differently from me. He showed me how to sell professionally. He taught me the right questions to ask and the right responses to give. He explained that selling is a professional process, with a logical series of steps, from separating "prospects" from "suspects" through the process of developing rapport, identifying needs, presenting my product effectively, answering objections, closing the sale, and then getting resales and referrals from my satisfied customers.

I couldn't believe it! "You mean there is a logical, orderly process to professional selling?" I asked him. Yes, there was, and this process had been discovered and taught by all successful sales organizations and sales trainers for many years. But because I did not know this process, I wandered around in the wilderness of underachievement and frustration, as most salespeople and entrepreneurs do, trying to make ends meet, with no idea why some people were more successful than others.

The Law of Cause and Effect

What I learned from this early experience was the *law of cause and effect*. This is the great law of Western civilization, the foundation of the scientific method, and the reason for all discoveries and breakthroughs in mathematics, medicine, physics, biology, technology, invention, and even warfare. The law of cause and effect says that *there is a reason for everything that happens.* For every effect there is a cause, or more than one cause, whether we know what it is or not.

This means that if you can be clear about what you want to accomplish, in this case, financial success, you simply find one or more people who started off earning less than you and who are now earning twice as much as you and then you do exactly what they did to get to where they are. It is not a miracle.

Put another way, "Success leaves tracks." Success is not an accident. Failure is not an accident. Success is the result of doing what other successful people do, over and over, until you get the same result that other successful people get.

An average person, with few natural advantages or gifts, will run circles around a genius if he or she knows the law of cause and effect in his area of activity and the genius does not.

Find Out How Success Is Achieved

From that time onward, I have been almost obsessive about finding out the cause-and-effect relationships between any business I got into and financial success in that business. They are always there and I always found them.

Over the years, I have started, built, managed, or turned around 22 businesses. I have made more than a million dollars, and sometimes quite a bit more, in eight industries. In each case, I knew nothing at all about those businesses when I got into them. But I found out what you had to do to succeed in those businesses, and then I did it over and over, until I had mastered the essential skills. And the money followed afterwards, as naturally as water runs downhill.

> Whatever it is that you want to accomplish, in any business or in any area of life, hundreds of thousands and millions of other people have already paid the price in trial, error, and sacrifice to learn what you need to learn to be successful.

The good news is that *all the answers have been found.* Whatever it is that you want to accomplish, in any business or in any area of life, hundreds of thousands and millions of other people have already paid the price in trial, error, and sacrifice to learn what you need to learn to be successful. You don't need to reinvent the wheel.

Benjamin Franklin once said, "Men can buy their experience or they can borrow it. When you buy your experience, you pay full price in terms of time, treasure, and suffering. But when you borrow your experience, you capitalize on the sufferings and sacrifices of others. Unfortunately, most men prefer to pay full price."

Commit to Lifelong Learning

Over the years, I've read thousands of books and tens of thousands of articles. I have worked as a consultant, speaker or trainer for more than 1,000 businesses in 45 countries. I have trained more than 4 million people and created many thousands of millionaires in entrepreneurship, sales, and business management. And every person who writes or phones me says that, once they understood the principle of cause and effect in their businesses, success followed soon after.

You have heard of the 80/20 rule, the Pareto Principle. This rule, which dates back to 1906, says that 20 percent of your activities will account for 80 percent of your results, 20 percent of your products will yield 80 percent of your sales and 80 percent of your profits, and 20 percent of your customers will buy 80 percent of your products and services.

Change Your Thinking, Change Your Life

The 80/20 rule has a special application with regard to the psychology of business success. It says that 80 percent of your success will be determined by the way you think about yourself and your world. Your mind is very powerful. Your thoughts have an inordinate impact on everything that happens to you. This principle is beautifully stated in *A Course in Miracles*, "Nothing has any meaning except the meaning that you give to it personally." And "You give meaning to everything you see."

Doctor Martin Seligman of the University of Pennsylvania calls this your "explanatory style." He says that the way that you interpret things to yourself, either positive or negative, determines how you feel and react to those events. If you interpret a setback or difficulty as a "learning experience," your response will be positive and constructive. You will seek the valuable lesson within the experience. You will actually benefit and grow from a setback or temporary failure.

Fully 80 percent of your success as an entrepreneur and as a person will be determined by the way you think, and the way you think has been studied and written about for more than 5,000 years. Throughout history, certain immutable mental laws have been discovered and rediscovered, and taught in various ways, in various places, throughout the ages.

All religions, philosophies, metaphysics, psychology, and success are based on these laws. Here they are.

The Law of Belief

The law of belief says that, whatever you believe, with feeling or conviction, becomes your reality. William James of Harvard said, "Belief creates the actual fact." In the New Testament, Jesus says, "According to your faith it is done unto you."

Your strong beliefs, your innermost convictions, largely determine how you think, feel, and act, and the results that you get. If you have strong beliefs of optimism, confidence, and ultimate success, nothing will be able to stop you from ultimately achieving your goals.

If you have negative beliefs of fear, self-doubt, and inferiority, nothing can help you.

In a study of more than 500 successful men and women, most of whom started with nothing and eventually reached the top of their fields, it was found that their one common belief was that, no matter what happened, they would ultimately be successful. They had an unshakeable confidence in their ability to overcome all difficulties and finally succeed. They looked upon every setback or disappointment as a learning experience that helped them to do more of the right things later on. Because of this belief, they eventually became unstoppable.

No One Better, No One Smarter

The most common belief that people have that holds them back is that others are better or smarter than they are. Deep down inside, they believe, "I'm not good enough."

If you truly believe that people who are doing better than you are therefore better than you or more talented than you are, you will not try as hard to achieve your goals, and you will quit more easily.

The fact is that *no one is better than you and no one is smarter than you.* You have more talent, ability, and innate potential than you could use in 100 lifetimes. You can achieve any goal that you can set for yourself, if you want it enough and are willing to work hard enough. If someone is *doing better* than you at the moment, it is simply because

> You have more talent, ability, and innate potential than you could use in 100 lifetimes.

he or she has figured out the cause-and-effect relationships for success in that particular area before you have. And whatever someone else has learned, you can learn as well.

To succeed as an entrepreneur, you must absolutely believe that you have everything you need to overcome every obstacle and achieve any goal you can set for yourself. On the road to wealth, there will be many pitfalls, detours, disappointments, and temporary failures. But when you absolutely believe that you will eventually be successful, you will not allow anything to stop you. You will find a way to get over, around, or under any obstacle. When you believe 100 percent in your ability to succeed, you will become unstoppable. This is the first quality for success in entrepreneurship and business building.

The Law of Expectations

This law says, "Whatever you expect, with confidence, becomes your own self-fulfilling prophecy."

You get not what you want in life, but what you expect. You can never rise any higher than your expectations of yourself. And the good news is that you can manufacture your own expectations.

The rule is that you should always "expect the best." Expect to gain something from every experience and to learn something from every problem or difficulty. You should confidently expect that everything that is happening is a part of a vast universal plan to make you successful. You should expect that every person and every encounter contains something of value that can help you in one way or another.

To use this law properly, you should expect to be happy, healthy, and successful. Expect to be popular, persuasive, and effective. Expect to get the things you want and achieve the results you are aiming at. This attitude of "positive expectation," based on your absolute belief that you will be successful, will virtually guarantee that you will achieve your goals.

The Law of Attraction

This is one of the most powerful laws in the universe, written about as far back as 3,000 years B.C. In its simplest form, it says, "Like attracts like." Similar things and people attract each other.

The law of attraction says that you are a "living magnet." Your thoughts radiate out from you like energy waves and attract back into your life people and circumstances in harmony with those dominant thoughts. When you emotionalize a thought, with either desire or fear, you dramatically increase the rate of vibration of that thought and more rapidly attract into your life circumstances in harmony with it.

The most powerful way to activate the law of attraction in your favor is to constantly expect that everything that happens is part of a great plan to make you successful. When you think about, imagine, and visualize a positive, exciting outcome to any event, you create a force field of energy that attracts into your life ideas, opportunities, money, and people that help to make your goal a reality.

Many thousands of self-made millionaires, mostly entrepreneurs, have been interviewed to find out what they "think about most of the time." Their answer? Self-made millionaires think about financial success and financial independence most of the time. From an early age, they are focused on both earning and keeping money from the sales and profitability of their own companies.

This law of attraction is very powerful. It is also *neutral*. If you think positive, constructive thoughts about your personal and financial goals, you attract into your life the resources necessary to achieve them. If you think negative, destructive thoughts of fear and worry, you attract negative events and problems consistent with those thoughts. The choice is up to you.

As you read through *The Way to Wealth*, you will learn and absorb more and more of the most productive, profitable ideas ever discovered for business success. As a result, you will attract into your life the situations, circumstances, and experiences that you need to apply these principles and ultimately be successful.

The Law of Correspondence

This is my favorite law of all. It is a summary law of many of the other mental laws. In its simplest form, the law of correspondence says, "As within, so without."

This law says that your outer world will tend to be a mirror image of your inner world. Put another way, "Everywhere you look, there you are." You see your true self in every part of your life.

The law of correspondence says that your life is a mirror that reflects back to you your dominant thoughts, in every area. Your relationships on the outside are a reflection of the kind of person you are on the inside with regard to people. Your work, career, position, and financial situation are a direct reflection of your thought, preparation, and application to your business life. Your health, on the outside, is a direct reflection of your attitudes and behaviors toward diet, exercise, and rest.

The wonderful truth is that you can control only one thing in life—your thoughts! As Viktor Frankl, founder of Logotherapy, once wrote, "The last great freedom of a person is to be able to choose his attitude toward any given set of circumstances." You can decide what you are going to think about most of the time, and thereby control your entire life.

> The wonderful truth is that you can control only one thing in life—your thoughts!

Because only you can control your thoughts, you are in complete charge of your life. If you want to change anything in your life on the outside, you need only go to work to change your thinking on the inside. By the universal laws of mind, as you change your inner world, your outer world will change to conform to it.

The Law of Concentration

This law says, "Whatever you dwell upon, grows." Whatever you concentrate on increases.

When you concentrate on any subject, more and more of your mental powers become focused on that subject. When you think continually about success and financial achievement and you concentrate single-mindedly on becoming excellent at getting the results that are necessary for success, you channel your energies and become more focused and effective in that area.

It is said that "Life is the study of attention." Whatever you give your attention to controls the direction of your life. And you always pay attention to what is most important to you. When you continually think about the things you want and the person you want to be, you move more and more in that direction.

Of course, like all laws, this law is neutral. Like a double-edged sword, it cuts in both directions. When you concentrate on what you want, you get more of it. But when you concentrate and think about things that you don't want, they also increase in your life and your experience. This is why it is said, "Whatever you resist, persists."

These laws can help you or harm you, depending upon their application. These laws are like a loaded pistol in the hands of a child. They can be very dangerous to your happiness and success if they are misused.

Remember: your mind is very powerful. And the more

> Remember: your mind is very powerful. And the more you use it, the more powerful it becomes.

you use it, the more powerful it becomes. By tapping into and channeling your mental powers, you can create almost anything you want in life.

The Law of Superconscious Activity

This is perhaps the most exciting and powerful law of all. This law says, "Whatever you can hold in your mind on a continuing basis, you can have."

This law goes on to state, "Any thought, plan, goal, or idea that you can hold in your mind on a continuing basis must eventually be brought into reality by your superconscious mind."

The superconscious mind has been written about and talked about throughout all of human history. This law is the reason that "Whatever you want, wants you."

When you have a clear goal in your mind that you continuously repeat through affirmation and visualization, you set up a force field of energy that brings you everything you need to achieve that goal. You will attract people, ideas, and money into your life to make your goal a reality. Your superconscious mind will continually solve every problem and overcome every obstacle on the way to your goal, as long as your goal is clear.

Your superconscious mind will bring you ideas and inspiration, often experienced as "a blinding flash of the obvious," that contains exactly the solution you need at that time.

When you combine all the mental laws together—cause and effect, belief, expectations, attraction, correspondence, concentration, and superconscious activity—you will soon develop mental powers that will make you irresistible and unstoppable. They will then bring you everything you want in life.

These mental laws explain why average people with average backgrounds, limited educations, no advantages in life, and often new immigrants with limited language skills and resources, often go on to achieve incredible success, build large companies, and become extremely wealthy. It has little to do with what is going on on the *outside*; it has everything to do with what is going on on the *inside*.

The Law of Probabilities

Some people think that "luck" is a major factor in business success. In fact, failures almost always attribute their lack of achievement to "bad luck." They say, "Successful people are simply those who have had a lucky break."

The fact is that, because of the mental laws that govern the human universe, there really is no such thing as luck. Everything happens for a reason, whether you know the reason or not. Instead of luck, there is the law of probabilities.

Probability theory, which is taught in the business faculties of most universities, dates back about 300 years. What it says is that there is a probability that everything will happen. There is a probability that an airplane will crash. There is a probability that you will live to be 100. There is a probability that you will become rich. All of finance, economics, business, life insurance, and science of every kind are based on the law of probabilities.

Probability theory also says, "Probabilities can be calculated with tremendous accuracy, using proven mathematical techniques."

The Uncertainty Principle

The German physicist, Werner Heisenberg, won a Nobel Prize in Physics in 1932 for his breakthrough concept called Heisenberg's Uncertainty Principle.

This principle says that, in any group of molecules, using probability theory, it is possible to predict that a certain percentage of those molecules will act in a certain way. But his breakthrough, which led to his Nobel Prize, was his proof that you could never tell exactly *which* molecules they would be.

How does this apply to business and entrepreneurship? Of 100 people who start work at the age of 21, by the time they reach the age of 65, five of them will be wealthy, 15 will be well off, and the other 80 percent will be dependent upon pensions or relatives, broke, still working, or dead. But the uncertainty principle tells us that we do not know exactly which ones will be in which category with the passing of time.

The good news is that you can *influence* the probabilities of something happening to you by thinking and acting in a specific way. For example, you can dramatically increase the probabilities that you will be successful and wealthy in business by doing certain things that have been proven to work over and over again until you get successful results. And it will not be a matter of luck.

Throughout *The Way to Wealth* you will learn proven principles that are practiced by every entrepreneur who goes from rags to riches, from poverty to affluence, from frustration to the realization of his or her full potential. By applying these ideas every day in your business and financial life, you can dramatically increase the probabilities that you will become wealthy as a business owner.

Take Charge of Your Life

Perhaps the starting point of all success in business and personal life revolves around the acceptance of *responsibility*. This is a major issue that is continually debated, especially by people who blame their problems on their parents, their bosses, politics, society, or something else. There seems to be an irresistible tendency among unsuccessful people to see the reasons for their problems and difficulties as originating outside of themselves. They refuse to accept responsibility.

But the fact is that you are 100 percent responsible for the person you are, what you are, and everything that happens to you. Your parents may be responsible for providing for you up to the age of 18, but after that you are on your own. You are responsible for everything that happens to you from that moment onward.

In almost every book, article, and study of success, the principle of personal responsibility emerges right at the beginning. The first chapter of Stephen Covey's bestselling book *The Seven Habits of Highly Effective People* is on personal responsibility. The first chapter of Jack Canfield's bestseller, *The Success Principles,* is on personal responsibility. Throughout the ages, the hallmark of leaders and all other superior people is that they accept an inordinately high degree of responsibility for themselves, their lives, the people around them, and everything that happens to them.

Refuse to Blame or Make Excuses

With regard to business, money, entrepreneurship, and careers, you become an "economic adult" only when you take charge of your own life and refuse to blame anyone or make excuses for anything. You move to full maturity when you begin to see yourself as the primary creative force in your own life.

Weak people, nonleaders, those who suffer failure and frustration as adults repeatedly condemn, complain about, and criticize other people. They make excuses rather than making progress. They blame others for their problems rather than accepting responsibility. But because of this, they have only a limited future.

The hallmark of the successful entrepreneur, the person who eventually becomes wealthy by building a profitable business, is that he or she accepts complete responsibility for himself or herself, his or her business, and everything that happens, good or bad. He or she may not be "at fault" when cheated or mistreated by other people or when his or her business occasionally gets into trouble, but this person accepts complete responsibility for his or her actions and for everything he or she does afterwards.

> The hallmark of the successful entrepreneur, the person who eventually becomes wealthy by building a profitable business, is that he or she accepts complete responsibility for himself or herself.

The mark of the mature person is his or her level of "response-ability." This is the ability to respond positively, constructively, and effectively to the inevitable difficulties, crises of adult life, especially business life. To be a successful entrepreneur and launch yourself on the way to wealth, you must leave your excuses behind. You must accept complete responsibility for your choices and decisions and for everything that happens as a result of them, from this day forward.

Seven Secrets of Entrepreneurial Success

There are seven essential principles that you must practice as an entrepreneur throughout your business life if you are to achieve maximum success. They have been taught and repeated in thousands of books and articles over the years. Here they are:

1. Clarity—You must be absolutely clear about who you are and what you want. You need clear, written goals and plans for every part of your life. As Zig Ziglar would say, you must become a "meaningful specific" rather than a "wandering generality."

Begin with your *values*. What do you believe in and stand for? What is most important to you in life? What would you pay for, fight for, suffer for, and die for? What do you really care about?

Someone once wrote, "Until you know exactly what you would do if you only had one hour left to live, you are not prepared to live."

What is your *vision* for yourself and your future? What is your vision for your family and your finances? What is your vision for your career and your company? Peter Drucker once wrote, "Even if you are starting your business on a kitchen table, you must have a vision of becoming a world leader in your field, or you will probably never be successful."

What is your *mission* for your business? What is it that you want to accomplish for your customers? What is it that you want to do to improve the lives and work of the people you intend to serve with your products and services? You need a clear vision and an inspiring mission to motivate yourself and others to do the hard work necessary to achieve business success.

What is your *purpose* for your life and your business? Why do you get up in the morning? What is your reason for being? And here's a great question: "What do you *really* want to do with your life?"

Finally, what are your *goals*? What do you want to accomplish in your financial life? What are your family goals? What are your health goals? What difference do you want to make in the lives of others? And here is the best question: "What would you dare to dream if you knew you could not fail?"

The greater clarity you have regarding answers to each of these issues—*values, vision, mission, purpose,* and *goals*—the greater will be the probabilities that you will accomplish something wonderful with your life.

2. Competence—To be truly successful and happy, you must be very good at what you do. You must resolve to join the top 10 percent in your field. You must set excellent performance of the business task as your primary goal and then dedicate all your energies to doing quality work and offering quality products and services.

To be successful in business, according to Jim Collins, author of *Good to Great*, you must find a field that satisfies three requirements. First, it must be something for which you have a passion, something you really believe in and love to do. Second, it must be an area where you have the potential to be the best, to be better than 90 percent of the people in that field. Third, it must be the production of a product or service that can be profitable and enable you to achieve all your financial goals.

According to the Harvard Business School, the most valuable asset a company can develop is its "reputation." Your reputation is defined as "how you are known to your customers." And the most important reputation you can

> According to the Harvard Business School, the most valuable asset a company can develop is its "reputation."

have revolves around the quality of the products and services you offer and the quality of the people who produce and deliver those services and interact with those customers. Competence and character are everything.

3. Constraints—Between where you are and your goal, whatever it is, there will always be a constraint or *limiting factor.*

Your ability to identify the most important factor that determines the speed at which you achieve your business goals is essential to your success.

The 80/20 rule applies to constraints in your business. Fully 80 percent of the reasons that you are not achieving your goals as quickly as you want will be within yourself. Only 20 percent will be contained in external circumstances or people.

What are your constraints? What holds you back? What sets the speed at which you achieve your goals? And what one thing could you do immediately to begin alleviating your main constraint? This is often the key to rapid progress.

4. Creativity—The essence of successful business is innovation. This is the ability to find faster, better, cheaper, easier ways to produce and deliver your products and services to your customers.

Fortunately, almost everyone is a "potential genius." You have more intelligence and ability than you could ever use, even if you lived 100 years. Your job is to unleash this creativity and focus it, like a laser beam, on removing your obstacles, solving your problems, and achieving your goals.

The essence of creativity is contained in your ability to solve the inevitable problems and difficulties of business life. Colin Powell said, "Leadership is the ability to solve problems." Success is the ability to solve problems. And remember: a goal unachieved is merely a problem unsolved.

The way of the successful entrepreneur is to focus on the *solution* rather than the problem. Focus on what is to be done, rather than what has happened or who is to blame. Concentrate all of your mental attention on finding a solution to any obstacle that is holding you back from the sales and profitability you desire to build your own successful business. And the more you think about solutions, the more solutions you will think of. You will actually feel yourself getting smarter by focusing all of your energies in a forward direction, on what you can do to continually improve your situation.

5. Concentration—Your ability to concentrate single-mindedly on one thing, the most important thing, and stay at it until it is complete, is an essential prerequisite for success. No success is possible without the ability to practice sustained concentration on a single goal or task, in a single direction.

The simplest way to learn to concentrate is to make a list for each day, before you begin. You then organize the list by priority by putting the numbers one through ten next to each item. Once you have determined your most important task, begin immediately to work on that task, and then discipline yourself to continue working until that top task is 100 percent complete. When you make a habit of doing this, starting and completing your most important tasks each day, you will double and triple your productivity and put yourself solidly on the way to wealth.

> Your ability to concentrate single-mindedly on one thing, the most important thing, and stay at it until it is complete, is an essential prerequisite for success.

6. Courage—Winston Churchill once wrote that, "Courage is rightly considered the foremost of the virtues, for upon it, all others depend."

It takes tremendous courage to take the entrepreneurial risks necessary to become wealthy. In study after study, the experts have concluded that it is the courage to take the "first step" that makes all the difference. This is the courage to launch in the direction of your goals, with no guarantee of success. Most people lack this kind of courage.

The second part of courage, once you have begun your entrepreneurial journey, is the courage to persist. As Ralph Waldo Emerson once said, "All great successes are the triumph of persistence."

The word *entrepreneur* means to "one who undertakes the risks of a new venture in pursuit of profit." Fully 90 percent of the population will never have sufficient courage to launch a new venture, to start a new business, "to boldly go where no one has gone before."

> The word *entrepreneur* means to "one who undertakes the risks of a new venture in pursuit of profit."

You need, first of all, the courage to begin, to move out of your comfort zone in the direction of your goals and dreams, even though you know you will experience many problems, difficulties, and temporary failures along the way.

Secondly, you need the courage to endure, to hang in there, to persist in the face of all adversity until you finally win through.

When you develop these twin qualities, the ability to step out in faith and then to persist resolutely in the face of all difficulties, your success is guaranteed.

7. Continuous Action—Perhaps the most outwardly identifiable quality of a successful person is that he or she is in continuous motion. The entrepreneur is always trying new things and, if they don't work, trying something else. It turns out that most entrepreneurs achieve their success in an area completely different from what they had initially expected. But because they continually reacted and responded constructively to change, trying new methods, abandoning activities that didn't work, picking themselves up after every defeat, and trying once more, they eventually won through.

Top people, especially entrepreneurs, seem to have these *three* qualities. First, they learn more things. Second, they try more things. Third, they persist longer than anyone else.

The good news is that, because of the law of probabilities, if you learn more things, try more things, and persist longer, you dramatically increase the probabilities that you will succeed greatly. If you launch toward your goal and resolve in advance to never give up, your success is virtually guaranteed.

The Quality That Guarantees All the Others

Earl Nightingale once said, "If integrity did not exist, it would have to be invented as the surest way of getting rich."

In a survey of high school and university students, they were asked what they wanted to do when they entered the world of work. Many of them made a similar statement: "I would like to go into business, but I don't want to have to do the things that businesspeople have to do in order to be successful."

For some reason, often supported by many teachers with an anti-business attitude, partially because of the various Enron and WorldCom-type scandals reported by the newspapers, there are many people who believe that much of business is based on dishonesty of some kind.

Nothing could be further from the truth! All business relationships are built on *trust*. Since all of business involves money—from bankers, suppliers, vendors, shareholders, and investors—and the opinions of customers and clients, the most important single ingredients for success in business are trust and credibility. The reputation of the company, its products and services, and the people who work in it is the most precious asset that a company can have and develop over time.

The Core Value

In every strategic planning session that I have done for companies, large and small, we begin with an exercise in *values clarification*. We ask, "What are the core values of this business?" And in every case, without exception, the first and foremost value that everyone agrees on unanimously is "integrity."

One time, after taking a group of senior company executives through this exercise and reaching the unanimous conclusion that *integrity* was the fundamental value of the business, the chairman of the company spoke up with an interesting observation. He said,

"It seems to me that integrity is not so much a value, but rather it is the value that *guarantees* all the others."

Truer words were never spoken. Honesty, trust, reliability, dependability, integrity, and truthfulness are not only the foundations of a successful business, but they are the fundamentals of a successful life. They are the values that ensure that you will practice all the other values that you espouse.

> Successful businesspeople think long term. They think about their reputations. They never do or say anything that is dishonest or untruthful.

In business and in life, there will always be temptations to cut corners and take advantage of the situation. But successful businesspeople think long term. They think about their reputations. They never do or say anything that is dishonest or untruthful. They behave as if they expect to be in business for 20 years or longer. And successful people know that trust and integrity are perhaps most important than anything else.

Always Be True to Yourself

When you embark on *The Way to Wealth*, you should be prepared for many ups and downs along the way. You will have good days and bad days, good years and bad years. You'll have time of profit and times of loss, times of success and times of temporary failure. But to be successful in the long run, you must make the decision, in advance, that you will never compromise your integrity for anything. As Ralph Waldo Emerson wrote, "Nothing is at last sacred but the integrity of your own soul."

There are 25 million businesses in America. Probably 99.99 percent of those businesses are run and operated by men and women of character, people who tell the truth and live the truth. As a result, bankers lend them money, customers buy their products and services, people work for them for many years, and they sleep well at night. Integrity is the quality that makes all of this possible.

The Right Attitude for Success

The final part of the psychology of business success has to do with your attitude toward work. You have heard it said, "The harder I work, the luckier I get." The fact is that your willingness and ability to work hard for many months and years are indispensable to your success in business.

When Thomas Stanley and William Danko were doing their interviews for *The Millionaire Next Door*, they often asked self-made entrepreneurial millionaires the secrets of their success. The answer that they got back, thousands of times, was similar: "I didn't start off with a fancy background or good education; I was just willing to work harder than anyone else."

Michael Jordan, who was once cut from his high school basketball team for being lazy, resolved that it would never happen to him again. Later he said, "Everyone has talent, but ability takes hard work."

The 40-Plus Formula

Over the years, I have developed what I call my "40-Plus Formula" for success. This formula says that, if you only work 40 hours a week, all you do is survive. All you have is a job; all you will ever be is "just over broke."

On the other hand, every hour that you put in over 40 hours each week is an investment in your future success. You can tell with unerring accuracy where you are going to be in the years ahead by how many hours you are putting into your work above and beyond the normal workweek.

The average entrepreneur and self-made millionaire in America works 59 hours a week. At the beginning of their careers and their businesses, they often work 70, 80, and 90 hours per week, seven days a week, sometimes for several years, before they break through.

There is no substitute for hard work. The harder you work, the luckier you get. By the law of probabilities, if you work longer and harder than the average person, you are going to achieve more, and soon vastly more, than the average person.

This is why it is vital that you love what you do. It is only when you love your work, your products and services, your customers and your staff that you will be able to maintain the energy, drive, and persistence to overcome all obstacles.

The great secret to success is to "do what you love to do, and then become very good at doing it."

You must love what you do so much that you are willing to throw your whole heart into it, month after month and year after year. You must believe, from deep in your heart, that your product or service is good and valuable and important for your customers. You must commit yourself totally to doing what you do in an excellent fashion and to continuous personal improvement.

The Ultimate Reward

My friend Jim Rohn once said, "The greatest reward in becoming a millionaire is not the amount of money that you earn. It is the kind of person that you have to become to become a millionaire in the first place."

To *have* more, you must first *be* more. For you to set out on the way to wealth and become a self-made entrepreneurial millionaire, you will have to develop many qualities at a higher level than you ever have before. You will have to become an exceptional person. You will have to become *more* than you ever imagined possible for you.

To realize your full potential and to achieve all your financial goals in your own business, you will be required to develop the virtues of integrity, courage, and persistence to a much higher level than you have up until now. You will have to practice the qualities of clarity, competence, creativity, concentration, and continuous action until they are as natural to you as breathing in and breathing out. You will have to accept complete responsibility for your life and everything that happens to you, and especially for the way you think in every area.

When you develop these qualities and become a completely different person, you will eventually achieve all your goals in life, including financial success. The best part of becoming an extraordinary person is that, if something happens and you lose it all, it won't really matter. Because you have become a different person, you will then be able to make it all back again, and more, far faster than the first time.

Welcome to *The Way to Wealth*. You are about to embark on a grand adventure that may last for the rest of your working lifetime. But if you have the courage to begin and the persistence to endure, nothing can hold you back from achieving all your goals and dreams. If you decide that, no matter what, you will never give up, you will eventually become unstoppable.

Action Exercises

1. Decide exactly what you want in life in each area and write it down. Make your goals clear, specific, and measurable.

2. Identify the most important skill that you could develop to move you into the top 10 percent of people in your field. Then do something immediately to begin developing that skill.

3. Identify the major constraint or limiting factor, inside yourself or in your world, that is setting the speed at which you achieve your most important goal. Begin working on removing that constraint today.

4. Determine your biggest single problem or obstacle in your business or personal life. Then focus all your time and attention on the possible solutions.

5. Make a list of what you would want to be, do, and have if you had no limitations, if you were absolutely guaranteed of success.

6. Accept complete responsibility for your life. Refuse from this day forward to make excuses or blame anyone for anything. Instead, take action to make your goals a reality.

7. Continually reaffirm and visualize your goals of financial success, excellent health, and personal happiness as a reality. Remember: the person you *see* is the person you will *be*.

CHAPTER TWO

Planning for Success

Action without planning is the cause of every failure.

—Peter Drucker

---

here is a rule that "before you do anything, you have to do something else first." The first thing you have to do in business is to plan, and plan again, and keep planning until your plans work consistently to get you the results you want. The major reason for business failure is, first, failure to plan in advance and, second, failure to revise your plans if they do not work for some reason. Failing to plan is planning to fail.

What is the highest-paid work in business? Answer: *Thinking!* Thinking is the highest-paid work because of a special factor called "consequences."

You can always determine how valuable and important something is by measuring the potential consequences of doing it or not doing it. The potential consequences of having a cup of coffee or chatting with a coworker are virtually zero. It does not matter at all whether you do them or not. But the consequences of planning, of thinking through your actions before you begin, can be enormous. They can make all the difference between success and failure, poverty and wealth, happiness and unhappiness, a life of affluence or a life of despair.

Everything you are or ever will be is the result of your choices and decisions. Your choices and decisions have brought you to where you are today. If you are not happy about your current situation, then you must make new choices and better decisions for the future. There is no other way. And thinking is the essential ingredient in both choices and decision-making.

The Ten Keys to Business Success

There are ten critical areas where your ability to think largely determines the success or failure of your business. The greater clarity you have in each of these areas, the better decisions you will make and the better results you will achieve.

1. Key Purpose. What is the purpose of a business? Many people think that the purpose of a business is to earn a profit, but they are wrong. The true purpose of a business is to create and keep a customer. Profits are the result of creating and keeping a sufficient number of customers cost-effectively.

> Fully 50 percent of your time, efforts, and expenses should be focused on creating and keeping customers in some way.

Fully 50 percent of your time, efforts, and expenses should be focused on creating and keeping customers in some way. The number-one reason for business problems is the failure to attract and keep a sufficient number of customers at the prices that you need to charge to make a profit and grow your business.

2. Key Measure. The key measure of business success is *customer satisfaction*. Your ability to satisfy your customers to such a degree that they buy from you rather than from someone else, that they buy again, and that they bring their friends is the key determinant of growth and profitability.

What is the most important sale? It is the second sale! You can acquire customers initially through discounts, special offers, and even deception. But it is only when the customer buys for the second time that he or she proves to you that you have delivered on your promises and satisfied his or her expectations. The second sale is the true measure of customer satisfaction.

3. Key Requirement. The key requirement for wealth building and business success is for you to *add value* in some way. All wealth comes from adding value. All business growth and profitability come from adding value. Every day, you must be looking for ways to add more and more value to the customer experience.

You can add value in many ways—increasing quality, lowering costs, accelerating delivery, improving customer satisfaction, satisfying customer needs faster, better, or cheaper than your competitors. The ways you can add value are only limited by your imagination.

The one thing that all customers buy, no matter what the product or service, is "improvement." Your goal must be to improve the life or work of your customer in some way, and continue doing so, more and more. By adding value, you create enough value so that you can keep some for yourself. This is called profit.

4. Key Focus. The most important person in the business is the *customer.* You must focus on the customer at all times. Customers are fickle, disloyal, changeable, impatient, and demanding—just like you. Nonetheless, the customer must be the central focus of everything you do in business.

Sam Walton once said, "We have only one boss, and that is the customer, and he can fire us at any time by simply buying from someone else."

The two great rules for business success are: Rule Number One—The customer is always right—and Rule Number Two—If ever you are in doubt, refer back to Rule Number One.

5. Key Word. In life, work, and business, you will always be rewarded in direct proportion to the value of your *contribution* to others, as they see it. The focus on outward contribution, to your company, your customers, and your community, is the central requirement for you to become an ever more valuable person, in every area.

Every day you must be looking for ways to increase the value of your contribution. You must be looking for ways to do your job and satisfy your customers better, faster, or cheaper.

Everything you learn that you can apply to increase the value of your contribution increases the value of your life and your rewards.

6. Key Question. The most important question you ask, to solve any problem, overcome any obstacle, or achieve any business goal is *"How?"*

Most things that you try in business won't work, at least the first few times. All of business life is a process of trial and error. Over and over, you must ask, "How can we do this? How can we solve this problem? How can we achieve this level of sales and profitability? How can we overcome this obstacle?" Top people always ask the question *"How?"* and then act on the answers that come to them.

> Top people always ask the question *"How?"* and then act on the answers that come to them.

7. Key Strategy. In a world of rapid change and continuing, aggressive competition, you must practice *continuous improvement* in every area of your business and personal life.

As Pat Riley, the basketball coach, said, "If you're not getting better, you're getting worse."

Never be satisfied. Dedicate yourself to "continuous and never-ending improvement" (CANEI). Practice the Japanese method of *kaizen*, which means "continuous betterment."

Continually seek faster, better, cheaper, easier, and more efficient ways to generate leads, make sales, produce products and services, deliver them satisfactorily, and satisfy your customers so that they come back and buy, again and again. By continuously improving what you are doing, in every area, you will eventually become one of the leading businesses in your industry.

8. Key Activity. The heartbeat of your business is *sales*. Dun & Bradstreet analyzed thousands of companies that had gone broke over the years and concluded that the number-one reason for business failure was "low sales." When they researched further, they found that the number-one reason for business success was "high sales." And all else was commentary.

Morning, noon, and night, the best brains, talents, and energies of your business must be focused on generating more and better sales from more and better customers. My motto, whenever I have faced a business slowdown or financial problem, has always been *"When in doubt, sell your way out!"* This should be your guiding principle as well.

> My motto, whenever I have faced a business slowdown or financial problem, has always been *"When in doubt, sell your way out!"*

All successful companies have well-organized sales systems, which they improve continuously, every single day. From the time you start in the morning, you and your whole company must think about and work on sales all day long.

9. Key Number. The most important number in business is *cash flow*. Cash flow is to the business as blood and oxygen are to the brain. You can have every activity working efficiently in your business, but if your cash flow is cut off for any reason, the business can die, sometimes overnight.

As a business owner, you must keep your eye on the cash at all times. Focus on cash flow. Think about cash flow. Ask questions about cash flow. Never allow yourself to run out of cash, no matter what hard decisions you have to make or sacrifices you have to engage in. Cash is king.

10. Key Goal. Every business must have a *growth plan*. Growth must be the goal of all of your business activities. You should have a goal to grow 10 percent, 20 percent, or even 30 percent each year. Some companies grow 50 percent and 100 percent per year, and not by accident.

The only real growth is profit growth. Profit growth is always measurable in what is called "free cash flow." This is the actual amount of money that the business throws off each month, each quarter, and each year, above and beyond the total cost and expense of running the business.

You should have a growth plan for the number of new leads you attract and for the number of new customers you acquire from those leads. You should have a growth plan for sales, revenues, and profitability. If you do not deliberately plan for continuous growth, you will automatically stagnate and begin to fall behind. Growth is not an accident. It is something that is planned and pursued every single day.

11. Key Quality. The most important quality to ensure your success is your level of *determination*. Even though it takes a good deal of courage to start a new business, more than two million people make this leap each year. But initial courage is not enough.

As soon as you start a new business, you immediately begin to experience unexpected problems, setbacks, reversals, obstacles, and even temporary failure. When you hit the wall in your business, it will be your level of determination that will see you through.

One of the most important techniques I ever learned was the power of mentally programming yourself in advance of the problem or setback, even when you do not know what it will be. The way you do this is to say to yourself, *"No matter what happens in my business, I will never, never give up."* Repeat this over and over.

By programming your mind with this command, when you unexpectedly hit the unavoidable speed bumps of life, you will be psychologically and emotionally prepared to bounce back and keep on going. But if you have not preprogrammed yourself, you will be in danger of hesitating and even giving up when the going gets rough.

12. Key Result. When you apply the first 11 keys to your business life, the result you will enjoy is the success and financial independence you set out for in the beginning.

Your ultimate goal in business is to reach the point where you have enough money so that you never have to worry about money again. This is called "the number."

> Your ultimate goal in business is to reach the point where you have enough money so that you never have to worry about money again.

How much will you need to acquire before you know that you have enough and that everything else you earn is icing on the cake? For each person, the number will be different. What is yours?

Start with Your Goals

In planning for success, you always start with yourself and your personal goals. Remember: your work and business life are means to an end. They are the things that you do so that you can enjoy the most important parts of your life—your family and your relationships.

Fully 85 percent of your happiness in life will come from your relationships with other people. The greater clarity you have about what is really important to you, the better decisions you will make in both your business and personal life.

Remember the great question: *"What do I really want to do with my life?"* If you could wave a magic wand and be, do, or have anything at all in life, what would you choose for yourself? If you had all the time and money, all the friends and contacts, all the knowledge and experience, and no limitations at all, what would you really want to do with your life?" This is the true beginning of personal strategic planning.

The 20/10 Exercise

Use the "20/10 Exercise." Imagine that you received $20 million cash in the bank today, tax-free. But simultaneously, you learned that you only had ten years left to live. If these two events happened simultaneously, $20 million cash plus only ten years to live, what would you choose to do with the rest of your life?

Who would you want to be with? Who would you no longer want to be with? What would you want to do? Where would you want to go? What would you like to accomplish? What sort of legacy would you want to leave? These are some of the great questions of life.

Practice the Quick List Method

In our Focal Point Advanced Coaching and Mentoring Program, we put our clients through a "Quick List" exercise where we require them to write down three answers in less than 30 seconds to each of the following questions. Jot down answers for yourself.

1. What are your three most important overall goals in life, right now?
2. What are your three most important family or relationship goals, right now?
3. What are your three most important business goals, right now?
4. What are your three most important financial goals, right now?

5. What are your three most important health goals, right now?

6. What are your three most important community and social goals, right now?

When you only have 30 seconds to write the answers to these questions, your answers will be as accurate as if you had 30 minutes or three hours. The answers that jump out at you with this 30-second exercise will usually be disturbingly accurate and will tell you immediately what is really important to you in each key area of life.

Your Major Definite Purpose

Here is a great question: *"What one goal would you set for yourself if you knew you could not fail?"*

Imagine that you could achieve any one goal, small or large, short term or long term. Imagine that you were absolutely guaranteed of success for that goal. Your only responsibility was to be absolutely clear about exactly what it is that you would want to be, have, or do more than anything else in the world. What would it be?

Once you become perfectly clear about who you are and what you want personally, you can then move on to setting your business and financial goals.

Your Plan for Your Business

Business planning is both simple and powerful. It takes time and discipline to sit down and think through the ingredients of your business plan, but the payoff can be extraordinary. And it is not the plan itself, but the process of thinking through and preparing the plan that is the most important.

After D-Day, General Dwight D. Eisenhower was asked about the year of planning that led up to the Normandy Invasion. He said, "The plan itself became useless as soon as we hit the beach, but the process of planning was indispensable."

Business planning is quite simple. It consists of three levels of accounting:

1. Top line: sales and revenues—projected and actual
2. Middle line: deduct all costs necessary to achieve the top line
3. Bottom line: the profit or loss from business activities

In business planning, you must think through and strive for maximum accuracy at each of these three levels and continually review them against actual results.

Four Key Numbers You Must Know

To plan intelligently, you must know the exact and total amount you receive for each product or service you sell, less all costs for discounts, breakage, loss, returns, shrinkage, service, and replacements. Many companies sell their products or services at a loss because they do not know exactly how much they actually receive after all expenses are deducted.

> To plan intelligently, you must know the exact and total amount you receive for each product or service you sell, less all costs.

The second number you must know is the total cost of selling your product or service. This includes not only the direct costs, or what is called "cost of goods sold," but the costs of marketing, advertising, promotion, sales commissions, and all other expenses related to the sale.

The third number you must know is the total and exact cost of your business operations. You must accurately calculate exactly how much it costs to run your business and to both acquire and support the top-line sales.

The fourth number you must know is the exact profit or loss that you earn each month and cumulatively, month by month, throughout the year. Inaccuracies in calculating profits or losses can lead to serious problems, and even the collapse of the enterprise.

Conduct a Profit Analysis

You should regularly conduct a "profit analysis" of every product and service that you sell. To do this, you calculate the exact net price that you receive from the sale of an individual product or service. You then deduct every single direct and indirect cost attributable to the acquisition, fulfillment, delivery, and service of that product. Finally, you calculate the exact profit to the penny that you earn from the sale of each of your products and services.

When you complete this profit analysis, you will find that all of your products and services can be organized along a scale or continuum from the most profitable to the least profitable.

When companies conduct this profit analysis for the first time, they are often astonished to find that certain products to which they paid little attention are the most profitable products that the company sells. They may not be high priced or high volume, but because they are so inexpensive to sell and deliver, each of them is highly profitable.

Many companies also find that some of their products that are high volume, which they advertise and promote in great quantity, are not making any money at all, or even losing money on every sale.

Think like a Turnaround Specialist

Whenever a company gets into trouble, which means that either sales or cash flow are down or declining, they bring in a "turnaround specialist." The first thing these professionals do is to conduct a cold-blooded analysis of the profitability of every product, service, and activity in the business. They then move immediately to cut out all loss-making parts of the business, discontinuing entire product or service lines, and shutting down factories and stores.

Surprise! Surprise! As soon as the turnaround specialist has ruthlessly cut all loss-making parts of the business and stopped the bleeding, the company surges back to profitability and everyone looks like a hero.

You should be acting as your own turnaround specialist in your own company on a regular basis, especially if you have any problem or concern about cash flow and profitability.

Strategic Planning Questions

There are seven questions that you must ask regularly as part of your strategic planning process.

1. What business are you in? What business are you *really* in? Define your business in terms of "what it does" for your customer rather than "what it is," your product or service.

> All customers care about is what your product or service does to improve their life or work in some way.

The fact is that customers do not care about your product or service. All they care about is what your product or service does to improve their life or work in some way. You must always define your business in terms of the positive change that your product or service brings about for the customer, because that is all that the customer buys.

2. Who is your customer? Who is your ideal customer? Who is your perfect customer? If you were to run an ad in the paper for perfect customers, how would you describe them?

Your ability to determine the perfect customer for what you sell is critical to your business. A mistake in this area can be fatal. Define your customer in terms of age, income, education, family status, industry, position, geographical location, and the specific attitudes, beliefs, and desires he or she would have at this moment to become a customer for what you sell.

3. Why does your customer buy your product or service? What value does he or she seek? What benefits does or she desire to enjoy? What change or improvement in his or her life does he or she seek? What is the exact reason that would cause a customer to buy from you immediately, rather than to delay the decision?

4. What is your competitive advantage? Your competitive advantage consists of one or more benefits that you offer your customers that no other competitor can offer. This is often called your "area of excellence" or "area of uniqueness."

Perhaps most important question of all is what is your *"unique selling proposition?"* This is the one thing that you or your company can offer a customer that no other competitor anywhere can offer to that customer. This is also something that your customer wants, needs, desires, and will pay for immediately at the price you charge. What is yours?

Jack Welch once said, "If you don't have competitive advantage, don't compete."

> Jack Welch once said, "If you don't have competitive advantage, don't compete."

Peter Drucker said, "If you do not have competitive advantage, you must immediately go to work to develop one."

What *will* your competitive advantage be in the future, if business continues as it is today? What *could* your competitive advantage be if you made changes or improvements in your product or service offerings? What *should* your competitive advantage be if you want to be the best in your field? These are the key questions that determine your business success.

5. Who is your competitor? Who does your ideal customer buy from rather than buying from you? What advantages or benefits does your customer perceive that he or she receives in buying from your competitor that he or she does not feel that you provide?

Most important of all, what could you do immediately to be equal or superior to your best competitor? What could you do to neutralize the perception of added value that your customer sees in buying from your competitor? It is only when you can defeat your competitor in the heart and mind of your customer that you can survive and thrive in business.

6. What are the constraints that hold you back? If your goal is to double your sales and profits over the next two or three years, what is holding you back from achieving that goal? Why aren't your sales already twice as high *already*?

In every business situation and business strategy, there is a major constraint that sets the speed at how rapidly you achieve your goal. Your ability to identify this constraint accurately and then to focus your time, energy, and intelligence on alleviating this constraint can make all the difference between business success and failure.

7. What are the 20 percent of activities that you can engage in that could account for 80 percent of your results? Who are the 20 percent of your customers who account for 80 percent of your business? What are the 20 percent of your products that account for 80 percent of your sales? What are the 20 percent of your products, services, and customers that account for 80 percent of your profits?

Sometimes, you can transform your business results by simply eliminating all low-value, no-value activities. The natural tendency of businesses is to offer too many products, to too many customers, at too many price points, in too many markets. As a result, they disperse their energies and end up spending most of their time on low-value, low-profit activities.

Starting Over Again Today

If you were starting your business over again and you had to focus all your energies on selling just one or a few products or services, which ones would you choose? Which customers would you dedicate yourself to serving better and better? Which sales and marketing activities yield the best results?

Which people and processes are the most efficient and effective in your business? Where and how can you focus your time and attention to get better business results? These are the key questions in planning. The answers change continually as your business evolves and grows.

Finally, based on your answers to the questions above, what actions should you take immediately to build a more profitable business? What is the first action you should take? When are you going to take it? Who is going to be responsible? Whatever you decide to do, remember that action-orientation is the hallmark of successful entrepreneurs. Once they make a decision they move fast, without procrastination or delay. You must do the same.

The Power of the Business Plan

Developing a business plan before you begin forces you to think through each critical number and issue in your business. When you begin the process of developing a business plan, imagine that you are a management consultant and that you have been hired at a high hourly rate to come in and develop this business plan for your company. As your own management consultant, you must be fastidiously correct, objective, and honest about each number.

Perhaps the very best business planning software available in the world today is Business Plan Pro from Palo Alto Software. This "fill-in-the-blanks" software guides and prompts you to put every critical number in its proper place. It enables you to change numbers as you get better information and to immediately incorporate those numbers throughout the business plan, changing your top line, middle line, and bottom line simultaneously.

Before computers and the Internet, I would spend many hours with a spreadsheet constructing my business plans painstakingly by hand. Now, with the miracle of this world-class software, you can save yourself countless hours and thousands of dollars producing a business plan that is more accurate and easier to use than ever before.

The Benefit of Planning

A group of business researchers did a study a few years ago. They interviewed the presidents and executives of fast-growing businesses about their uses of the business planning process. They selected two groups of 50 companies each, one group of companies that had developed a complete business plan before beginning operations and one group of companies that had begun business operations without a written plan and then simply reacted and responded as they went along.

After two years, they went back and interviewed these companies again. Companies in the first group, which had developed complete business plans before operations, had been successful overall, and some extraordinarily successful. Only one company that had started with a business plan had gone out of business in the two-year period.

Of the companies that started without a business plan, fully 49 had gone broke over the last two years. Like starting off across a foreign country with no road signs or road maps, they had become hopelessly lost, bogged down, and eventually gone out of business.

TABLE OF CONTENTS

Executive Summary

Section 1.0. The Concepts

Section 2.0. Objectives

Section 3.0. Market Analysis

3.1. General description of the entire marketplace for the product or service

3.2. Precise description of segment(s) to be pursued

3.3. Description of intermediate influences on buyers such as dealers, distributors, sales representatives, associates, etc.

3.4. Competitive conditions—present and anticipated

3.5. Pricing conditions—present and anticipated

3.6. Governmental influences—present and anticipated

3.7. History of similar products, services, or businesses

3.8. Breakeven point estimates, i.e., how many units and/or how much of the market has to be sold to cover costs?

Section 4.0. Production

4.1. Equipment requirements

4.2. Facility requirements

4.3. Raw material, labor, and supplies: requirements and sources

4.4. Quality control, packaging, transportation, etc.: requirements and sources

4.5. Program for initial time period

4.6. Schedule—Who is to do what by when (Exhibit)

4.7. Budget (Exhibit)

4.8. Results expected (Exhibit)

4.9. Contingency plans

Section 5.0. Marketing

5.1. Method(s) of selling and advertising to be employed

5.2. Product or service features and benefits to be emphasized

5.3. Program for initial time period

5.4. Schedule—Who is to do what by when (Exhibit)

5.5. Budget (Exhibit)

5.6. Results expected (Exhibit)

5.7. Contingency plans

Section 6.0. Organization and People

6.1. Who is accountable for whom, for what? Structure (Exhibit)

6.2. Staffing program for initial time period

6.3. Schedule (Exhibit)

6.4. Budget (Exhibit)

6.5. Results expected (e.g., brief position description)

6.6. Contingency plans

Section 7.0. Funds Flow and Financial Projections

7.1. Complete statement of expected sales and expenses for the next sales period (Exhibit)

7.2. Pro forma profit and loss statements (Exhibit)

7.3. Pro forma balance sheets

7.4. Program for monitoring and controlling funds with people and systems included in the organization planning

Section 8.0. Ownership

8.1. Summary of funding requirements

8.2. Form of business—partnership, corporation, etc.

8.3. Program for raising equity and/or debt money required, if any

8.4. Projected returns to investors

Planning Forces You to Think Better

The surprising part of the study was when they asked the heads of the successful companies how closely they had adhered to their business plans once they had been designed. In almost every case, they said that, once the business plan was complete they had put it into a drawer and seldom looked at it again until the beginning of the next year, when they drew up a new business plan.

They said almost unanimously that the value of the business plan was that it forced them to think through and back up every number and assumption of their planned business activities for the coming year. This forced them to be more accurate and thoughtful about how, when, and where they were going to generate the necessary sales, how they were going to produce and deliver the products and services, and how they were going to pay for the operations of their businesses.

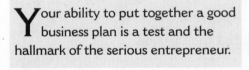

Your ability to put together a good business plan is a test and the hallmark of the serious entrepreneur.

Your business plan is the key tool that you use to plan your business life. Your ability to put together a good business plan is a test and the hallmark of the serious entrepreneur. A company without a business plan is like a ship without a rudder. It drifts from day to day and simply reacts and responds to the turbulence and winds that sweep back and forth on the seas of business life.

Guide to Preparing a Business Plan

These are the issues and questions that you must ask and answer in the process of creating your business plan. Unfortunately, most entrepreneurs have not conducted this analysis and are just guessing at most of the answers.

Note: *If technology is an important ingredient in the success of the enterprise, a separate section, Technology, should be included in the business plan. Such a section would include details on staffing and methods of inquiry and testing as well as schedules, budgets, results expected, and contingency plans. A section on Technology would normally be inserted after Section 5.0, Marketing.*

Systematize Your Business Activities

Your business will be successful, generating steady, predictable sales and cash flow, to the exact degree to which you develop systems that put as much of your business on autopilot as possible.

A system is a step-by-step process, from beginning to end, that you use to ensure consistency and dependable performance in every area.

Every new business or business activity requires tremendous time, effort, expense, and even "genius" to learn and develop for the first time. But once the system has been developed, through trial and error, it can eventually be systematized to the point where the business activities can be carried out by ordinary people. Until a business activity is systematized, it exists largely in the mind of the individual who knows how to do it. As a result, it cannot be duplicated or replicated. If the person who knows how to do the job is not there, the business can eventually grind to a halt.

The Systems You Need

1. Lead Generation. You need a proven system of marketing, advertising, and promotion that generates a steady steam of qualified leads, whether phoning your place of business, responding on the Internet, or personally coming into your store to buy your product or service. Without this continuous and predictable stream of leads, your sales and revenues will dry up and your cash flow will slow to a trickle, threatening the survival of your business.

2. Lead Conversion. You need a proven sales system to convert interested prospects into buying customers. This system begins with a sales script that every customer service representative and salesperson uses from the first contact with the prospect through to the completed sale.

The use of a preplanned sales script can *triple* your sales almost overnight.

The use of a preplanned sales script can *triple* your sales almost overnight. By using a sales script, each person who answers the phone, calls on a customer, or greets a customer walking in the door knows exactly what to say from the first greeting through to the final purchase.

Your sales system will be developed as the result of trial and error. As you evaluate your sales process, you will find that there are things that you do and say that are effective and others that are not.

Over time, you will smooth out the rough spots in your sales process, machining and polishing the words and actions so that you turn interested prospects into buying customers over and over again.

3. Production of the Product or Service. You need a proven system, from beginning to end, for producing the product or service that you have sold to the customer. This proven system will ensure consistency of quality, ease of operation, efficiency of activity, and continually lower costs of production and delivery as the system improves.

4. Delivery System. You need a step-by-step system to fulfill orders and deliver the product or service to the customer in a timely fashion. This system enables you to get your product or service to the customer quickly and efficiently with minimum delays and with a high level of quality.

5. Service Systems. You need written policies and procedures for follow-up service to each of your customers, including established ways to handle customer needs and complaints, to generate additional sales, to keep in regular customer contact, to elicit referrals and recommendations from satisfied customers to new customers, and to alert your customers of new products and services that they may be interested in buying.

6. Accounting Systems. You need smoothly functioning accounting systems that track every penny of revenue and expense coming into or moving out of the business. Fortunately, there are computer programs for small and large businesses that you can use to keep track of all financial flows in your business so you will always know your proper financial status.

7. Hiring, Training, and Personnel Systems. You need written systems that clearly describe each job and how it is to be done. In addition, you need systems for training, development, and personnel relations. Each person who works for you must know exactly what he or she is expected to do and to what standard of quality. Your employees must understand the terms and conditions of their jobs, what is deemed unsatisfactory performance, and what are grounds for termination. They must know exactly what they are entitled to in terms of medical insurance, sick pay, vacation days, and other key elements of the work experience.

System Development

The way you develop systems is quite simple. You take a piece of paper and describe the job, step by step, from the first function to the last. List every task that must be completed to do the job well. You then review the job description with the people who are doing it to "debug" the process and ensure that it is accurate.

Once you have developed a complete description of a particular job or activity, it should be so clear that a new person can learn the job by simply following the system until he or she has memorized it and can do it automatically.

What is most important is that the details of the job are put down on paper rather than left in the mind and memory of the individual doing that job. The most important word in systems development is the word "replicability." Every job must be systematized and documented so that an ordinary person can replicate it by simply following the steps that you have written down.

> The most important word in systems development is the word "replicability."

Critical Success Factors, Benchmarks , and Metrics

The final part of business planning and setting up business systems is for you to determine measures, metrics, and scorecards for every job and for every part of every job.

These are often called *key success measures* or *critical success indicators*. These are numbers that you can attach to any activity to determine whether or not that activity has been carried out satisfactorily.

We often refer to *key result areas*, those specific results that must be achieved by each person in his or her particular job. Attached to each key result area is a *standard of performance*, a measure that tells the individual and the superior exactly how well that job has been done.

Your Economic Denominator

In every business, there is a critical number that is the key to the success or failure of the enterprise. Jim Collins, in his book *Good to Great*, calls this the "economic denominator." The economic denominator in a business is the number that most accurately measures and determines the success of that business.

In some businesses, the economic denominator is the number of prospects who phone for further information as the result of advertising and promotion activities. In other businesses, it is the number of prospective customers who walk in the door seeking information in order to decide whether or not to buy the product or service being offered. The economic denominator can be the number of sales that the company makes each day or the average size of the sales that are made on a daily basis.

The Measure of Success

Some years ago I built a shopping center, and I was seeking a restaurant as a tenant in a 6,000-square-foot part of the shopping center next to the supermarket and facing the parking lot. It was a prime location, and I soon found a successful pizza restaurateur, Peter, who was operating three successful restaurants in other communities.

Peter invited me to come with him one evening while he did his market research among the other pizza restaurants in the town. What I learned was that, whenever a pizza restaurant took an order, in person or over the phone, it would place the order stub on a spike on top of the cash register. When Peter did his market research, he simply walked into the restaurant, went up to the cash register, and did a quick count of the number of orders on the spike at 8 o'clock in the evening.

After we had visited three pizza restaurants on a Wednesday night, all with their spikes almost full of orders, he turned to me and said, "It's a deal. We can sign the lease agreements tomorrow." He subsequently built and opened a new restaurant in that location that became a tremendous success. I never forgot that "market research" experience. What is the equivalent of "orders on a spike" for your business?

What is your economic denominator? This is like the bull's-eye in the target that you are aiming at. What is the one number that more than anything else indicates the financial health of your business?

Personal Standards and Goals

Each person in your business should have an economic denominator as well. He or she should have a key success indicator or metric to determine whether or not he or she is doing the job in an excellent fashion. This number should be clear, visible, and objective. Everyone should know what it is and be able to determine whether or not he or she is reaching that number regularly. This is the answer to the question, "How do I measure success at my job?"

Remember the Basics

In business, there are three basic activities: market and sell the product or service, produce and deliver the product or service that you have sold, and manage and administer the money and activities of your business. Whenever a company runs into trouble, it is because of a problem in one or more of these three critical areas.

At the beginning of this chapter, I said that the highest paid work in business is *thinking*. Your ability to gather the information necessary to create a complete business plan and to think through the critical issues of your business will have greater consequences in determining your success or failure than any other factor.

Action Exercises

1. Resolve today to begin the hard work of planning, of thinking through and writing down your answers to the key questions asked in this chapter. Get Business Plan Pro and fill in the blanks.

2. Define your product or service in terms of what it does for your customer, how it improves his or her life or work.

3. Determine your key competitors and why it is that your potential customers buy from them, rather than from you.

4. What are the 20 percent of your sales and marketing activities that could contribute 80 percent of the value of all the work you do?

5. What could you do, starting today, to become one of the very best companies in your industry?

6. Determine your exact cash flow projections for the coming year and your cash requirements to stay in business.

7. Think on paper. Take the time to set down on a regular basis and review the key numbers and data discussed in this chapter.

CHAPTER THREE

Selecting the Right Product or Service

Nothing splendid has ever been achieved except by those who dared to believe that something inside them was superior to circumstance.

—Bruce Barton

I N ITS SIMPLEST TERMS, THE KEY TO BUSINESS SUCCESS IS "HIGH sales." The reason for business failure is "low sales." All else is commentary.

Your ability to select the right product or service for you and for your company, your market, your customers, and your future is the critical determinant of your sales, success, and profitability. You must give this area a lot of thought. Wherever you see a business that is not succeeding, you see a business that has selected a product or service that people either do not want or are not willing to pay for at the price that is being demanded.

In Chapter 1, I mentioned that companies become successful when they find a product or service that fits three key parameters. First, it is a product or service that the company owners, founders, and executives passionately believe in. Second, it is a product for which the company has the potential to be the best, to be in the top 10 percent of the market. Third, the product or service is profitable. If the company is successful in bringing it to market and selling it in sufficient quantity, the company will earn substantial profits.

Reasons for Mediocrity

Wherever you see a business in trouble, you will find a weakness in one of these three areas. First, the people in the company are neutral or even negative to the products and services they sell. As a result, they don't really care that much for their customers. They are simply going through the motions each day with no passion for the importance or goodness of what they do.

The second reason that companies fail is because their product offering is not good enough. It is a "me too" product. There are lots of competitive products that are equal to or even better at the same or even lower price. For this

> One rule for business success is that you should only offer a product or service, or enter into a market, where you feel that you can be the best sometime in the future.

reason, it is always hard to sell and to get repeat business.

One rule for business success is that you should only offer a product or service, or enter into a market, where you feel that you can be the best sometime in the future. You should continually ask, "How can we be the best at what we do?"

Third, when a business gets into trouble, it is often because its profits are too low. In most cases, it is selling a product or service at such a low price that the company can barely survive. The need to sell at a low price can be the result of poor quality, poor marketing, intense competition, low demand, or better alternatives.

Choosing What You Are Going to Sell

To find a product or service, begin with yourself. Do you like it? Would you use it? Would you sell it to your mother or your best friend? Do you feel that the product is so good for others that you are prepared to sell it for 10 or 20 years?

Think like a customer. Would a customer like it? Would a customer buy it? Would a customer buy it from you rather than buying it from a competitor? Why or why not?

Wal-Mart has become the most successful retailing operation in the world. One of the reasons for this is because every buyer for Wal-Mart stores sees himself or herself as working directly for the customer. His or her job is to negotiate the prices down and the quality up for the products that Wal-Mart stores will carry. Every buyer feels engaged in a noble quest to get Wal-Mart customers the very best for the very least.

Even if you are already in business, it is important for you to remember that 80 percent of the products and services you are selling today will be obsolete and off the market within five years. In addition, most of what people will be consuming in five years does not even exist today. Research, development, and introduction of new products and services are vital to your success.

Think About the Future

In their bestselling book on strategy, *Competing for the Future,* authors Gary Hamel and C. K. Prahalad point out that top businesses and businesspeople think five years into the future. They imagine that five years have passed and they look around and ask, "What will our customers be wanting or buying in five years?"

Top entrepreneurs practice "back from the future" thinking. They project forward and then think backward. They then imagine the steps they will have to take, in the present, to be ready for the customers and the markets of tomorrow.

As Peter Drucker said, "The very best way to predict the future is to create it."

What are the trends? In what direction is your business moving? What is it that customers are using today that they were not using five years ago? Since customers are impatient, fickle, demanding, and disloyal, and they always want the very most for the very least, what sorts of products and services will they be demanding from you in five years? Your ability to think ahead and then to take the necessary steps to be ready for the inevitable future is a mark of the superior businessperson.

> As Peter Drucker said, "The very best way to predict the future is to create it."

Reinvent Yourself Regularly

A great exercise for you is to practice what is called "reinvention." Imagine reinventing yourself and your business every six months, based on the knowledge you have at that time.

If your business were to burn to the ground or if you were to lose your job unexpectedly and you could then choose to do anything you wanted, what would you do differently from today?

Use the "walk across the street" method of strategic planning. If you could walk across the street and start your business over again today, what would you do more of or less of? What would you get into or get out of? What would you start up or stop doing altogether? What products and services would you immediately bring to the market and what products or services would you no longer offer?

No Limits to New Product Ideas

There are many ways to find new products and services. Because of the "perfect storm" of information explosion, technology expansion, and increased competition, more and more products and services are pouring into the market from both national and international competitors. Since there are no limits to human wants and desires, there will never be an end to products and services produced to satisfy those wants and desires.

Many of the great fortunes of today are based on products, services, and technologies that did not exist 25 years ago. Most of the great fortunes of tomorrow will be based on products, services, and technologies that are not yet in the market. You must be open, aware, and alert to business opportunities happening all around you.

How to Find a New Product or Service

1. Read everything you can find. You've heard the old saying, "Fish where the fish are." If you are looking for new products, services, or business opportunities, read the magazines and newspapers where they are offered. Read all the trade magazines in your field and in business in general. Read all the business magazines, newspapers, publications, and even newsletters in your area of interest. Subscribe to everything that you can find. Don't be cheap or lazy in this area.

Sometimes, one idea in one specialty publication in your field of business can save or make you a fortune if you recognize it and act quickly.

For example, in one of my businesses, we saw a story about an automatic recreational vehicle washing bay. The concept had been developed by a mechanic in Arkansas and he was looking for people to license the concept nationwide.

Normally, it takes about two hours to wash an RV, from top to bottom. It usually takes one or two people using long-handled brushes and hoses to soap down and rinse the sides and top. With an automatic RV washing bay, the entire job can be done in nine minutes and the vehicle is cleaner than if one or two people took two hours to wash it.

We bought a license for the technology, set up the RV wash bay on our property, put out the word in the local market, and within one year we were generating more than $25,000 per month in sales with a gross profit of more than 80 percent.

2. Attend trade shows, fairs, and exhibitions in your field. In reading newspapers and magazines, you will learn about trade shows being held all over the country in your area of specialization. Currently, there are more than 5,000 trade shows per year.

The people who attend these trade shows are there to demonstrate the latest breakthroughs in products or services. They are seeking to make direct sales to professional buyers and to find licensees for their products in other markets. You can learn more about what is going on in your industry by walking around the floors of a trade show for a few hours than you could if you read, reviewed, and asked questions for an entire year.

3. Read the business press. Look for new product or service ideas that are being featured as news stories. Read *Forbes, Fortune,* and *Business Week.* Read *The Wall Street Journal* and *Investor's Business Daily.* Read the business and business opportunity sections in your local newspaper. Be prepared to look at a lot of opportunities before you find the right one for you.

My friend Dolf de Roos, author of *Real Estate Riches,* teaches people how to buy houses with no money down. He uses what he calls the "100-10-3-1 Formula."

He says that, at the beginning, you have to look at 100 houses before you will find ten houses on which you can make a "no money down" offer. Of those ten offers, only three will counteroffer with acceptable prices and terms. Of those three, you negotiate and purchase only one.

This gives you a ratio of 100:1. It seems like a lot of work, but I've spoken to many people who say that this formula is quite predictable. If they look at 100 homes, they will end up buying one home at an excellent price that they can fix up and resell or rent out for more than their total cost of purchasing and carrying the house. If they do this once per month, they can eventually become skilled enough to buy 12 houses per year with little or no money down. People who do this systematically can build up a substantial estate in residential housing.

A friend of mine in Dallas used this formula to buy 66 houses over a period of three years. He made more than three million dollars when he sold them all and moved onto his next venture.

My point is this: you may have to look at dozens of business opportunities and new products or services before you find the right one for you, but if you keep looking and exploring, the law of probabilities says that you must eventually find something that fits into your plans and your budget.

4. Keep your eyes open while you are traveling. Many new product or service ideas are never sold outside of their home markets, local, national, or even international. Many people have become wealthy by seeing a product for sale while traveling overseas, inquiring and getting the rights to distribute it exclusively in the U.S. or in their market area, and starting a successful business as a result.

> Many people have become wealthy by seeing a product for sale while traveling overseas, inquiring and getting the rights to distribute it exclusively in the U.S.

Fully 95 percent of products manufactured and sold successfully in foreign countries are never sold overseas. The main reason is that the manufacturers or producers of these products are so busy making their businesses successful at home that they have no time or ability to expand into other markets.

Consulates and embassies of many nations include economic divisions, the purpose of each being exclusively to promote trade between the country that it represents and other countries. These economic divisions of the consulates and embassies carry catalogs, brochures, and information from manufacturers of products seeking distribution in other countries.

You can often find a tremendous product opportunity by simply phoning or going online to contact the foreign services offices of countries like China, Taiwan, Korea, Germany, the Netherlands, France, Britain, and Italy.

There are dozens, maybe hundreds, of products that are well made, attractive, and selling well in their home markets. Often you can get the exclusive rights to distribute these products simply for the asking.

5. Study demographic trends. In his book *Innovation and Entrepreneurship*, Peter Drucker says that one of the major sources of new product and services ideas is demographic trends.

Akio Morita, co-founder of Sony, discovered a new product in this way. His children and grandchildren were continually playing boom boxes around the house, seemingly unable to go anywhere without listening to their loud music. Morita, in a fit of exasperation, began wondering if it was possible to develop a technology that would enable people to listen to their music without disturbing other people around them.

He brought this challenge up to his engineers at Sony Corporation. As a result, they came up with the Sony Walkman. They took technology that had developed far enough so that they could produce high-quality music in small earphones connected to radios and other audio players. The Sony Walkman went on to become one of the best and most profitable product launches in history, eventually leading to the Apple iPod of today, which sold 70 million sets in its first three years on the market.

Keep your eye open for trends in consumer tastes, of all ages and incomes. There are trends in health and fitness that you can capitalize on. There are trends in aging and senior citizen requirements. The baby boomers, 78 million strong, the most affluent and educated generation in history, have decided that they want to live forever and be beautiful and fit. This is creating unlimited opportunities for people who can provide health and fitness products, vacations and leisure activities, resort and retirement communities, and a variety of other products and services. Could there be an opportunity in these demographic trends for you?

6. Look into your own field or skills. Remember the "acres of diamonds" concept: what you are looking for may be right under your feet. It may be within your own knowledge, education, experience, interest, or current job. You may have a million-dollar idea staring you right in the face.

Be Prepared to Take Action

The most important thing is to get started in some way. Most businesses succeed in unexpected ways, offering products or services different from what they originally anticipated. Very often, they find that a product or service they had brought to market does not work, but with some modifications it develops into a different product or service that works for a different customer.

> Most businesses succeed in unexpected ways, offering products or services different from what they originally anticipated.

The key is to do your homework, identify a potential product or service market, and then launch quickly. As soon as you launch, you will immediately get feedback that will enable you to correct your course, modify your product or service, and make it more acceptable to a larger customer base.

Determine Your Costs

Once you have an idea for a product or service, you must find out exactly how much it will cost. You must determine the direct costs of acquiring or producing the product or service, plus all of the indirect costs of marketing, selling, and running the business for that product or service. It comes as a shock to some business people to learn that you can go broke with a 100 percent markup. You can pay $100 for a product that you can quite comfortably resell at $200 and still lose money.

By the time you have calculated the actual cost of the product, and added in the costs of marketing, advertising, selling, shipping, delivery, breakage, loss, pilferage, and product returns, you will often be amazed at how your margin has shrunk. Then you have to calculate the costs of opening and operating an office, with staff salaries, rents, utilities, telephones, transportation, travel, postage, computers, and a dozen other factors, all of which are essential to getting the product to the customer satisfactorily.

Conduct a One-Customer Market Test

Once you have a clear idea of your costs and the price that you must charge in order for it to make sense to go into this business in the first place, you should do a "one-customer test."

Phone or visit a prospective customer for the product or service you are thinking of bringing to the market. Ask if he or she would buy it. If so, how much would he or she pay for it? If you could produce it and deliver it for a certain amount, how many would he or she purchase?

Don't Be Secretive

Some people think that they must be secretive about a new product or service. This can often lead to a disaster.

A friend of mine was on a business trip to Hong Kong. He went to a toy store to get a gift for his son and found a "creepy crawly" spider-like toy that, when you threw it against the wall, would stick and then walk down the wall, just like a spider.

He became very excited about this toy. He bought one and then contacted the Taiwanese manufacturer. The Taiwanese manufacturer offered to make him a distributor for the U.S. if he purchased a minimum of 10,000 units at $3 apiece.

This was in June. He immediately signed the agreement, borrowed and scraped together $30,000, and ordered 10,000 units, without telling anyone. His goal was to receive delivery by August or September and then sell them in large quantities to department stores, toy stores, and other outlets for the Christmas season.

As soon as he took delivery and had 10,000 units in storage, he phoned the buyer for a large department store chain and told him that he had a "fantastic new toy product that would sell like hot cakes at Christmas time." The buyer invited him to come in and demonstrate the product. When he arrived, full of excitement, he took the toy out of his briefcase and threw it against the wall, where it promptly walked down the wall, exactly as it was supposed to.

"What do you think of that?" he asked.

The buyer said, "It looks fantastic! We could sell thousands of these during the Christmas season."

"But, as it happens, we are already carrying that product. We have purchased them in quantity from a Taiwanese manufacturer for $1.59 each. How much are you asking for yours?"

It turned out that the Taiwanese manufacturer had arranged distribution rights for numerous companies throughout the U.S. and Canada, each of which were purchasing 100,000 or more and getting rock-bottom prices. My friend was both shocked and dismayed. He had estimated that the product could be sold for $4.95 each. But the department stores were planning to sell them for $2.99—exactly his cost price.

Needless to say, he lost most of his money. The mistake that he had made was not testing the market thoroughly in advance by going to a potential buyer and getting an immediate opinion.

> Most people in business are so overwhelmed with their day-to-day responsibilities that they have no time or interest in someone else's ideas.

Some people say, "If I tell someone else about my idea, they will steal it." Don't worry. This seldom happens. Most people in business are so overwhelmed with their day-to-day responsibilities that they have no time or interest in someone else's ideas. They are working full time just to be successful with their current products and services.

How to Do Fast, Cheap Market Research

Before launching your product or service or any new business venture, you must spend considerable time in research. The pay-off will be in excess of 10:1 in the time saved and the money saved or earned.

First, find out every detail of the product or service. Make yourself an expert. Go onto the Internet and Google the product or service. Explore every outlet or source of information on it. Imagine that you are going to be grilled by venture capitalists or bankers and you must be able to demonstrate a thorough knowledge of every detail.

Second, read all the trade magazines, articles, and stories on the business industry or service. Sometimes one observation in a current magazine or article can be critical to business success or failure.

Third, seek out people in the same business and ask their opinion of the product or service. If you are thinking of buying a business, go and talk with everyone who is already in that business and ask them what they think. Would they get into the business again if they were starting over today? What advice or counsel would they give someone who was interested in getting into this business?

You will be absolutely amazed at how open and helpful people are when you ask for their advice. They are not secretive at all. And sometimes they can open your eyes to possibilities or pitfalls that you would never have seen on your own.

Take your product or service to your bank manager for his or her opinion or advice. Even if you do not have a company bank account, you have a checking or savings account. Your bank manager is talking with businesspeople who have ideas for new products and services every single day. Often, he or she will have observations, or even internal banking publications, that can give you ideas and insights that are priceless. Don't be afraid to ask.

Fourth, ask your family, friends, and acquaintances for information, ideas, and opinions. Especially, listen to the women in your life. They are the very best shoppers around and they now make or control the majority of buying decisions in America.

When you take your product or service to a woman, she will give you an immediate, honest, accurate, and intuitive answer about its attractiveness and marketability. In addition, most women know a lot about what else is available and how to compare your product or service against alternatives. If a woman is negative to your product or service idea, you should immediately pull back and see if it is possible to change it to make it more attractive.

Fifth, visit prospective customers for the product or service and ask if they would buy it. Prospective customers are an extraordinarily good source of market information. If you ask them their opinion of your product or service, they will tell you immediately. They will not hold back. And they are almost always accurate. They will give you insights and feedback that you could not get by hiring a market research firm to go out and poll hundreds or thousands of people.

> Visit prospective customers for the product or service and ask if they would buy it. Prospective customers are an extraordinarily good source of market information.

Finally, in doing fast and cheap market research, investigate all competitors for the product or service. Who else is offering a competitive product or service? What are its special features or benefits? And especially, ask, "Why would someone switch to buy from me?"

Apply the Rule of Three

There is a marketing principle called the Rule of Three. This rule says that your product or service must be superior in at least three ways to any competitive product or service in your market. It must be faster, better, cheaper, easier to use, of higher quality, more convenient, or superior in some other way. But you must have at least three reasons for a person to switch from his or her current product or service to yours. What are they?

This is not to say that you cannot enter the market and defeat your competitors with your new product or service. But remember: your competitors are usually very determined and more experienced than you. They will be very aggressive about protecting their markets and their customers. They will upgrade or otherwise modify their offerings, cut their prices, increase their services, and do everything they can think of to frustrate your desire to enter the market. You must be prepared for what is called "competitive response" whenever you try to sell anything to anyone who is already purchasing it from someone else.

Determine the Size of the Market

In analyzing your competitors, you must find out exactly how much of your proposed product or service they are selling currently. Is this market fixed, growing, or declining? If the market is fixed, you are going to have to take away market share from people who are determined not to give it up.

If the market is declining, which means that there are fewer customers for this product or service each month and each year, you should think carefully about whether to venture into that industry.

If the market is growing, you must determine by how much and what you can do to get a reasonable share of this expanding market.

How Much Can You Charge?

You must find out exactly what your competitors are charging, how much customers are actually paying, and what the total, aggregate size of the market is.

In many cases, you hear claims that competitors are selling large amounts of a product or service for a particular price. But when you do your homework, you find that the actual quantity of sales is much lower and the price that they are actually getting from the customer is considerably less than the amount they are advertising or charging initially. This reality can considerably change or skew the economics of getting into this business.

"Does" vs. "Is"

Here is an important fact that I will repeat again and again. No one really cares about your product or service.

No one cares what it is. No one cares about how it was developed or the technology that went into it. Nobody cares about you or your company or your history or background. Nobody cares about you or your product or service at all.

All that people care about is what the product does for them. Customers buy one thing and one thing only—improvement. Customers buy a product or a service only when it is absolutely clear to them that it will improve some aspect of their life or work cost-effectively.

Economists say that every human action is an attempt to relieve a "felt dissatisfaction." The customer must feel, or be made to feel, dissatisfied, discontent, or unhappy with his or her current situation and simultaneously see that purchasing your product or service will relieve this feeling of discontent.

People buy in anticipation of being better off because of your product or service than they would have been without it.

People buy benefits, not products. People buy solutions to their problems, not services. People buy in anticipation of being better off because of your product or service than they would have been without it.

Customers buy the feeling that they anticipate enjoying after buying what you are selling. You must be crystal clear about how your product or service will improve their situation and their emotions before you think of bringing your product or service to market or writing the first word of advertising or sales copy.

The Great Marketing Question

Here is the great question that you must ask and answer continually throughout the life of your business. This larger question includes every small question to which you must know the answer. Whenever you have a problem in your business, of any kind, it is because one of these questions has not been answered or has been answered incorrectly. Here it is:

> "*What* exactly is to be sold, and *to whom* is it to be sold, and *how* is it going to be marketed, advertised, and sold, and *by whom*, and at *what* price and terms, and *how* is it to be manufactured, produced, and delivered, and *how*, and *by whom*, and under *what* conditions, and *how* is it to be serviced to ensure complete customer satisfaction leading to resales and referrals?"

This is the great business question, and it must be broken down into its component questions.

1. What is to be sold? You must answer this question in terms of what it *does* for your customer, how it benefits him or her, what problems it solves, and the specific improvement that it brings about in your customer's life or work.

2. To whom is it to be sold? Who is your customer, *exactly*? What are his or her age, education, income, family status, job, occupation, industry? Where does your customer live? When does he or she buy? What else is he or she buying today? And why would that customer buy from you?

3. How is it to be sold? You must determine the exact sales process, from the first customer contact—whether face to face, on the Internet, or on the telephone—and the exact words that will be used, step by step, to identify customer needs, present the product or service as a solution to his or her needs, answer objections, close the sale, and get the customer to commit to the purchase.

4. By whom is it to be sold? You must be absolutely clear about the individuals who will be responsible for the direct contact and sales activities, converting an interested prospect attracted by your advertising into a paying customer. The failure to clearly identify and train salespeople is a major reason for business underachievement and failure.

4. What marketing, advertising, and promotional activities will you use? How will you generate leads and attract prospective customers? What media will you use to advertise and promote your product or service? How much will it cost? How effective will it be? How many leads do you expect to generate for the amount of money that you intend to spend generating them? How will you position your product or service against your competitors to get people to call or come to you rather than to go to them?

5. How much will you charge? Exactly what will your prices be, not only for an individual sale, but for volume sales, wholesale, discount sales, and sales in combination with other products or services? Your ability to correctly determine the proper prices for your products or services is an art and a science and it can be critical to your success.

6. How is the product or service to be produced and delivered to your customer? What will it cost and how long will it take to produce the product or service once it is sold? How much will you have to invest? How much money will you have tied up in inventory before you make the first sale and generate revenues? In what way will you deliver the product or service to your customer satisfactorily so that he or she is happy with his or her purchase?

7. How will the customer pay for the product? What prices and terms will you offer? Will you require full payment in advance or part payment, or will you offer 30-, 60-, or 90-day terms of purchase? What are the standards in your industry? What sort of prices and terms will you have to offer to get the business? How could you revise these prices and terms to make them more satisfactory to yourself and your business?

8. How will you service the customer after the purchase? What steps will you take to make sure that your customer is so satisfied that he or she will buy again and refer you to others? Your customer service policy is the linchpin of your business. You 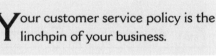 can succeed only to the degree to which people are satisfied to such an extent that they buy again and tell their friends.

You should sit down and think through the answers to these questions. Each time you have a slowdown or difficulty in sales, you should revisit these questions to make sure that your answers are accurate and acceptable to your prospective customer market.

Three Choices for Every Customer

Remember: customers always have three choices with regard to their money. First of all, they can buy from you. Second of all, they can buy from someone else. Third of all, they can refuse to buy at all at this time.

Customers have an infinite ability to put off the purchase decision. You must be absolutely clear why someone should buy your product or service from you, at this time, rather than from anyone else. If you are not crystal clear about the answer to this question, it is very difficult for you to market and advertise, to sell, to persuade your customer to make an immediate buying decision.

Customers always consider not only your products and services and the products and services of your competitors, but also alternative uses of the same amount of cash. Remember: customers buy the anticipation of how they will feel as the result of making the buying decision. If a customer feels that he or she will be happier or more satisfied by buying another product or service, then that is what the customer will do. You must make it clear that the highest and most immediate level of satisfaction that the customer will enjoy will come from buying your product or service at this moment.

Key Marketing Concerns

There are three final questions that you must ask with regard to your product or service.

First, is there *really* a market for what you want to sell? Are there customers who have needs that are not yet being satisfied, that you can satisfy with your product or service? Can your product or service be better in at least three distinct ways than anything else that is available to your prospective customers?

> Can your product or service be better in at least three distinct ways than anything else that is available to your prospective customers?

It is amazing how many people bring a product or service to market without determining whether or not there are actually customers who will buy the product or service, in that form, at that price.

Second, is the market *large enough*? Just because one or two people say that they would buy your product or service, this does not mean that there are enough customers to make this business a good use of your time and cash. Very often, friends and current customers will tell you that they would like you to offer a particular product or service. This can get you thinking about offering it. But you must be realistic and objective. You must determine that the market is large enough, and growing, for you to invest your time and money in this area.

Third, is the market *concentrated enough* so that you can reach it with the marketing methods and advertising media available? There may be a potential market of hundreds or thousands for your product or service, but if those potential customers are spread out evenly across the country, it may be cost-prohibitive for you to reach them.

On the other hand, the Internet may enable you to reach a narrow but deep market niche cost-effectively. But you must be sure that there are advertising and promotional media available that will enable you to contact prospective customers and convey to them that your product or service is available and that they should buy it immediately.

Remain Flexible

Fully 80 percent of all products and services in the marketplace today will be obsolete within five years and will be replaced with new products and services that are more satisfactory to the customers of the day. Fully 80 percent of new products and services brought to the market each year will fail. They will be the wrong products or services, at the wrong prices, for the wrong markets, at the wrong time, with the wrong competition. Products and services fail for a hundred reasons. This simply goes with the territory.

> Fully 80 percent of all products and services in the marketplace today will be obsolete within five years

You must be in a constant "new product development" mode. You must be continually scanning your marketplace and thinking of new, better, cheaper, more efficient, or easier products and services for your customers of today and the customers of tomorrow.

In every case, you should look at your products and services as an outsider, as a management consultant that you have hired at great cost to evaluate your business. Before you become emotionally involved or excited about a product or service, you must subject it to careful market testing, especially customer testing.

Your ability to select the right product or service and market it at the right price to the right customer base and sell it in the right quantity is the key to your success in business. You must make every effort to make sure that you get this part of your business right and that you continually improve in this area.

Action Exercises

1. What exactly is your product or service, in terms of how it benefits, helps, or improves the life or work of your customer?

2. Who is your exact customer, your ideal customer, your perfect customer, in terms of age, income, location, position, education, and specific situation or need?

3. How are you going to attract ideal customers in terms of advertising, promotion, and other lead-generation activities?

4. How are you going to sell your product or service, in terms of convincing a skeptical prospect that he or she should buy from you, right now?

5. How do you produce, package, ship, and deliver your product once you have sold it, to ensure a high level of quality?

6. How will you follow up and service your customer to ensure a high level of satisfaction and repeat business?

7. What is your plan to develop or discover new product or service ideas so that you can continually increase your sales and profitability?

CHAPTER FOUR

Marketing, Selling, and Customer Service

The longer I live, the more certain I am that the great difference between the great and the insignificant is energy; invincible determination, a purpose once fixed, and then death or victory.

—Sir Thomas Fowell Buxton

O NCE UPON A TIME, AT A COMPANY SEMINAR WITH A ROOMFUL of senior accountants, I asked, "How many people here are in sales?"

They say that accountants choose accounting because they lack the *charisma* of engineers. The very idea of selling is uncomfortable for them. They see themselves as high-level professionals, not as "salespeople." No one raised their hand.

I smiled at the group and then asked again, a bit more slowly and distinctly, "How many people here are *really* in sales?"

This time, one of the senior partners got it. He raised his hand. The others looked at him with some amazement. Then, one by one, they all got it. One by one, they all raised their hands. It had dawned on them that, even though they were accountants, they were all in sales.

Their personal success and the success of their company were totally determined by their ability to develop and maintain good business relationships with their clients. Every customer interaction was important; it either helped or hurt. Every time they met with a client, they were either building higher-quality, longer-term relationships or they were tearing them down. They were all in sales in some way.

Then I asked, "How many people here are in customer service?"

This time there was a certain degree of hesitation, but not as long as before. One by one, they began smiling at each other and tentatively raising their hands. Soon, the entire room of senior accountants had their hands up. It was clear to all of them that each person was in the business of sales and customer service from the time they started in the morning until they finished in the evening.

> The way to wealth is paved by sales and customer service. You should be spending 50 percent or more of your time in these two areas.

The way to wealth is paved by sales and customer service. You should be spending 50 percent or more of your time in these two areas. If someone asks you what you do at your company, you can say, "I am in charge of *new business development* and *customer service.*" From morning to night, your job is to find and keep customers for your company. Customers are everything.

The Purpose of a Business

At the beginning of each strategy session, I ask the question, "What is the purpose of a business?"

Almost invariably, people answer, "To make a profit!"

Then I'll point out gently that that is not quite correct. As Peter Drucker said, "The purpose of a business is to create and keep a customer."

All of the activities of a successful business are focused and concentrated on creating and keeping customers. When you are successful at creating and keeping customers in a cost-effective manner, the result will be a profit. But the profit always comes after the creation of the customer.

What is the key measure of business success? It is only one thing: customer satisfaction.

How do you measure customer satisfaction? Answer: repeat business.

What is the most important sale? Answer: the *second sale*. You can get the first sale by advertising, discounting, or free offers. But it is only when the customer buys the second time that he or she is telling you that you have satisfied

> It is only the second sale that is the true measure of how well you are doing in business.

the promises that you made to get him or her to buy from you the first time. It is only the second sale that is the true measure of how well you are doing in business.

Three Keys to Successful Sales

On the way to wealth, you have three goals in your business.

Your first goal is to get the customer to buy from you, rather than from anyone else, for the first time.

Your second goal, by delivering excellent products and services and giving excellent customer service, is to get the customer to buy from you again and again.

Your third goal, and the key to long-term business success, is to get your customer to bring his friends and to encourage them to buy from you as well. This is what happens with the very best companies in every business and industry.

The Customer Is Your Business

The most important person in your business is the customer. Your predominant consideration must always be the customer. You must think day and night about who your customers are, how to find them, and how to get them to buy. The customer is everything.

Tom Peters, whose book *In Search of Excellence* became one of the best-selling business books of all time, was asked some years later what he considered to be the most important of the eight business principles discussed in his book. He replied immediately, "An obsession with customer service."

To build a successful business, your central job is to create customers—to organize your business to produce products and services in such a way that people buy from you, buy again, and tell their friends. It is the one true measure of how well you are doing.

Marketing vs. Selling

Marketing and selling are two separate activities. Marketing is the process of *lead generation*. Marketing embraces everything you do up to the point of sale. The design, development, and determination of the exact product or service that you are going to sell are the first part of marketing. The second part is to think through every element of the *marketing mix* before you begin. These elements are *product, price, place, promotion, packaging, positioning,* and *people.*

> Marketing is the process of *lead generation*. Marketing embraces everything you do up to the point of sale.

1. Product/Service. What exactly is your product or service? What does it do for your customer? How does it improve his or her life or work? What products or services are you going to offer? What products or services are you not going to offer?

Any change in the product or service offered can dramatically change the entire nature of your business.

2. Price. How much are you going to charge for your product? Will you sell wholesale or retail? If you give volume discounts for large purchases, how much will you charge at that time? How do your prices compare with those of your competitors? Are they higher or lower? How do you justify your prices, whatever they are?

Any change to your pricing strategy can have a dramatic effect on your sales results and profits.

3. Place. Where exactly are you going to locate your business? Where are your customers? Do you sell from a retail storefront or by telephone and Internet from your offices?

Any change in the location of your business activities, the place where you make contact with your customer, can change the nature of your business.

4. Promotion. How do you advertise and attract customers? Once you have attracted potential customers, what is the specific sales process that you use to convert those prospects into customers? What systems do you use for developing and maintaining a successful sales process to get customers to buy from you?

5. Packaging. What do your product or service, place of business, and every other visual element of your company look like to your customers? Customers are extremely visual. They form their first impression about you and your company within four seconds of seeing you for the first time. Looking from the outside, is every part of the customer's visual experience with regard to your company excellent in every way?

Any change to the visual impact that your product or service makes on your prospect can have a dramatic effect on his or her behavior.

6. Positioning. How are you positioned in the minds and hearts of your customer? What words do your customers use when they talk about you and describe you to others? If your name were mentioned in a customer survey, how would customers and non-customers refer to you and your business?

The way people think about you and talk about you when you are not there is a critical factor that largely determines whether they buy from you or recommend you to their friends.

7. People. Who exactly are the people who interact with your customers? What do they look like? How do they dress? What do they say? What kinds of personality do they have? Prospective customers are largely emotional. They make most of their decisions based on the way they are treated by the people in your organization. What kind of "people experience" do customers have when they deal with you? How could it be improved?

Your Real Business

The starting point of business success, the first step on the road to wealth, is attracting potential customers. You can say that you are in the business of *customer acquisition*. In its simplest terms, the purpose of your advertising is to tell people that you have a product or service that they want and need and that you are the best choice for them at this time, all things considered.

To put it another way, you are in the business of "buying customers." Everything you do in your marketing, advertising, promotional, and selling efforts is aimed at buying customers at a cost that is lower than the profit that you earn from the sales you make. All promotional expenses have to be compared against this number.

Determine Your Profit per Sale

Before you spend any money acquiring customers, you must first determine your *breakeven point.* Your breakeven point is often called your *profit contribution*. This is the amount of profit that you make from the sale of each item. Once you have this number, you then determine how much you can afford to pay to acquire a customer, when every expense is added together.

For example, let's say that you pay $50 for a product and you sell that product for $100. Your profit contribution is $50 per item. That is the amount of profit that you make from each sale.

If you are contemplating spending $5,000 in advertising costs, you would calculate your breakeven point before you make a final decision: you would divide $5,000 by $50 to get a breakeven point of 100 units. This means that you would have to sell 100 units of your product in order to break even on that advertising expenditure. If you do not feel that you can generate 100 sales from an expenditure of $5,000, then this is not a good place for you to invest your advertising dollars. You are not in the business of losing money. You are in the business of making a profit from every investment, including every investment in advertising of any kind.

The Four Principles of Marketing Strategy

There are four keys to effective marketing strategy. Each of these principles must be thought through carefully and then continually revisited as the business grows and changes. Any changes in any one of these areas can have an enormous impact on the sales and profitability of the business.

Specialization

You must decide in exactly which area of your product or service market you are going to specialize. You cannot be all things to all customers. Too many businesses make the mistake of trying to offer too many products or services to too many types of customers at too many prices in too many ways. This is not the way to wealth.

You can specialize in three fundamental areas—product/service, customer/market, or geographical location.

You can specialize in a product/service area. This is what you do when you decide upon a single or a limited number of particular products or services that you are going to provide to your market. You can specialize in hardware, hot dogs, or hard-to-find books. Both you and your customer must be clear about your area of product/service specialization.

You can specialize in a specific customer or market. All-State Legal Supply of New Jersey specializes in law firms. It provides law firms with every product they need to operate efficiently. Wal-Mart specializes in serving customers who live from paycheck to paycheck. McDonald's specializes on providing fast food for people who want to eat quickly and conveniently. What customers do you specialize in serving?

You can specialize in a particular geographical area. This can be your neighborhood, your city, your state, the country, or the entire world. When you choose to specialize in a particular area, you are choosing not to offer your products or services outside that area.

This is often the case for franchise operations or for companies offering exclusive products and services in a particular market.

In business, deciding what to do is equally as important as deciding what not to do. When you are absolutely clear about your area of specialization, it is much easier for you to make decisions about the right and wrong products and services to offer to your customers.

Differentiation

This is perhaps the most important strategic marketing principle of all. All business success requires a differentiation of some kind.

All business success requires that you be both different from and better than your competitors in some clear, distinct way.

Your area of differentiation is called your *competitive advantage.* Your competitive advantage is what makes your product or service superior. It makes what you offer better than any other product or service offered by one of your competitors. Sometimes this is called your *area of excellence.* You develop a competitive advantage by becoming absolutely excellent in some area that is so important to your potential customer that he or she will buy from you rather than from someone else.

> You develop a competitive advantage by becoming absolutely excellent in some area that is so important to your potential customers.

Perhaps the most important part of competitive advantage is what I referred to before as your *unique selling proposition.* This is the one benefit that you offer for dealing with you that no competitor can offer. It is *unique.* No one else has it, in any way. It represents a value that customers are willing to pay for in comparison with the offerings of your competitors.

For a convenience store, the unique selling proposition (USP) could be nothing more than that the location is closer to the customer than another store selling similar products. For many companies, it is the warm, friendly people who sell the product or service and interact with the customers. For McDonald's or Starbucks, the unique selling proposition is the convenience of their locations, making it easy to get in and out.

If you don't have a competitive advantage, you must develop one of some kind. In addition, you must look into the future and determine what competitive advantage you will need in the months and years ahead to be seen as one of the best companies in your market.

Your goal is to offer products and services in such a way that you are seen to be in the top 10 percent of suppliers in your market. Your goal is to be "the best." The process of achieving competitive advantage requires a commitment to "continuous and never-ending improvement."

Segmentation

The third strategic marketing principle requires that you segment your market. You divide up your prospective customers into separate groups, based on the product or service area in which you specialize and the areas of superiority that you offer to prospective customers.

In market segmentation, you clearly identify those customers who are ideal for what you sell and who most appreciate and are willing to pay for those aspects of your product or service that make your offerings superior to those of your competitors.

In market segmentation, you begin with a description of your ideal or perfect customer. If you could wave a magic wand and attract the perfect customers, what would they look like? How would you describe them?

Who is your *ideal* customer? What is his or her age? Income? Education? Position or occupation? Industry? Geographical location? Type of family? Interests? Desires? Ambitions? Problems?

Once you have identified your ideal customer, this becomes your *target market*. You then ask questions such as "Where is my perfect customer? When does he or she buy? How does he or she buy? What value does he or she seek in buying from me? Of all the benefits my product or service offers, what is the one benefit that is most important to my ideal customer?"

Determine Your Competition

Who is your competition? Why doesn't your ideal customer buy from you? Why does your ideal customer buy from your competitor? What value does your ideal customer see in buying from your competitor that he or she does not see in buying from you? What could you do to offset this perception?

The business of creating and keeping customers is difficult, complex, frustrating, and time-consuming. Customers are demanding, fickle, disloyal, and unpredictable. They always want the very most for the very least and they want it immediately. They will abandon a supplier after buying from that person for 20 years if they perceive something better or cheaper across the street.

The only hope you have in acquiring customers is to focus most of your time and attention on determining exactly who they are, where they are, and what you have to do to get them to buy from you rather than from someone else.

Segment Your Market

If you offer more than one product or service, you will have to divide your potential customers into separate market segments. You will then have to identify the characteristics and qualities of prospective customers in each of these segments in order to advertise and sell to them effectively.

Keep asking, "Who are my customers? Where are my customers? Why do they buy? When do they buy? How do they buy? How can I get them to buy from me rather than from someone else? What value do they have to perceive that they will get from me that they will not get from anyone else?" Your failure to ask and answer these questions accurately can damage or even destroy their business.

> Keep asking, "Who are my customers? Where are my customers? Why do they buy? When do they buy? How do they buy?"

Concentration

Once you have applied the principles of specialization, differentiation, and segmentation to your products and services and to your customers and markets, you now have to *concentrate* your limited resources. You have to focus your time, energy, and money on those prospective customers that you have identified who are the most likely to buy from you the soonest.

In concentrating your resources, you identify the advertising media that are most likely to reach the people who are most likely to buy from you immediately.

Advertising Your Product or Service

As Steuart Henderson Britt said a half century ago, "Doing business without advertising is like winking at a girl in the dark; only you know what you are doing."

> **D**oing business without advertising is like winking at a girl in the dark; only you know what you are doing.

Advertising is an essential part of your customer-acquisition strategy. Advertising should be viewed as a form of sharing information. It is the way that you tell prospective customers that your product or service is available in a particular form, at a particular price, at a particular place, and for purchase in a particular way.

The good news is that effective advertising is *free*. Effective advertising yields you more profits than you would have had without advertising. Effective advertising has a high return on investment or profit per placement or insertion. Effective advertising more than pays for itself. This is your goal.

Determine How Customers Are Buying Today

There are various ways that you can advertise, depending upon what you sell and to whom you sell it. One of the best ways to determine your advertising strategy is to study your successful competitors. Find out how they advertise. Find out where they advertise repeatedly. If one of your competitors is advertising over and over again in a particular medium, that is usually proof enough that that advertising medium is succeeding in attracting customers in a cost-effective way. Don't reinvent the wheel.

Test and Measure

When you advertise, perhaps the most important principle is to test and measure—and then test and measure again. Most advertising doesn't work, at least initially. Many of the ads that you place will not attract a single customer. Many of the ads that you write for radio, television, newspaper, or Internet will achieve no results at all. You must continually test and measure your advertising results throughout your business career.

You may have to run five or ten different ads in five or ten places before you find an advertisement or medium that generates consistently profitable sales for you.

When you start or build a business, people who sell advertising of various kinds will call upon you. Most advertising that they will offer you will not work. Since your financial resources are always limited, you must be extremely careful in your allocation of every advertising dollar.

> Since your financial resources are always limited, you must be extremely careful in your allocation of every advertising dollar.

The Fallacy of Big Numbers

Always test on a small scale before you advertise on a large scale. Beware what is called the "fallacy of big numbers."

This fallacy suggests that if you take out an expensive advertisement of some kind that reaches 100,000 or 1,000,000 people, you will be sure to generate enough responses and sales to justify the cost. But what happens when people apply the fallacy of big numbers is that they spend enormous amounts of money on advertising that often attracts no response at all. And all of the money is lost.

There is an old saying: "Fully 50 percent of all advertising dollars are wasted. The problem is that no one knows which 50 percent it is." The sad fact is that the number of advertising dollars that are wasted can be much higher than 50 percent. It can be 80 percent, 90 percent, or even 100 percent. The only way to keep from making advertising budget mistakes is to test on a small scale and expand only when your small-scale tests turn out to be profitable.

Test on a Small Scale

If you are thinking of running a newspaper ad in a large daily paper, run the same ad in a neighborhood paper, at a much lower price. Your response rate will tell you quite quickly if the ad is going to work. Before you embark on a large radio advertising campaign, run the same ad, or three different ads, only three times. In each case, make an offer for your product or service and ask listeners to phone or visit your place of business. If you get no response from three radio advertisements, you will get no response from 30 advertisements.

Test and measure. Test and measure. Test and measure. Never stop testing and measuring. And find out what is working. Whenever a customer calls you or comes in, the second or third question out of your mouth should be "How did you hear about us?"

Whatever the customer says, write it down immediately. Keep an accurate tally of each customer response. If you listen closely enough to your customers, to the people who are actually responding to your advertising, they will tell you where to advertise.

Identify the Key Benefit

In addition, you can ask what it was about your advertising that caused the customer to visit you rather than to go somewhere else. In many cases, it was one benefit that you offered in your advertising that caused the customer to respond positively. If several customers give you the same answer, you can then design your future advertising around emphasizing this benefit for other prospective customers.

How to Write Effective Advertising

There are several keys to writing effective advertising.

Focus on One Thing

The first key is to focus on a single product, service, or benefit. Always imagine that a child is going to read your advertisement and then turn to another child and tell that other child what you sell and why someone should buy it from you.

Make your advertising simple, clear, and direct. Focus on a single reason why people should respond to the advertisement, rather than responding to the hundreds of other advertisements that they see and hear every day.

Focus on What Your Product or Service Does

Here is an unhappy little secret of business. I can't repeat it often enough. No one likes to admit it, but here it is again. Nobody cares about your product or service. Nobody cares what your product or service is. Customers care only about what your product or service does for them. Customers care only about how your product or service improves their life or work.

> Nobody cares what your product or service is. Customers care only about what your product or service does for them.

There are lists of reasons and motivations that cause people to buy. But you can boil them down into one single buying motivation: improvement!

Customers buy improvement, morning, noon, and night. All customers are concerned with is whether or not your product or service will improve their life or work in a particular way, right now. When you write an advertisement of any kind, the improvement you offer must be the focal point of your advertising. And it must be clear.

Call for Immediate Action

The second key to writing effective advertising is to tell the prospect exactly what action you want him or her to take immediately. "Come in today before 9:00 p.m. while supplies last!"

Here is an important rule: make it easy for your customer to buy from you. Be sure that your call to action is simple and easy to follow, especially on radio, where listeners have nothing to write on. Keep numbers to a minimum. They just confuse prospective customers.

Here is another rule: you do not try to *create a need* in your advertising. You only address a need that already exists, that the customer already has. You address a pain the customer already feels and wants to have taken away. You address a lack that the customer already experiences and offer to address it. You offer to provide a benefit that the customer already desires. Your goal is to use your advertising to talk to customers who already want what you are selling. The purpose of your advertising is to get the already qualified customer to buy from you rather than from someone else, and to buy now.

The Three-Part Formula for Effective Advertising

There is a formula for writing effective advertising, especially for radio and television.

First, you describe the problem the customer has, or the need the customer wants to satisfy, or the pain the customer wants to have taken away. This immediately grabs the attention of your ideal prospect.

Second, you describe the solution. You describe the ideal way to solve the problem, fulfill the need, or remove the pain. This triggers buying desire in the prospect's mind.

Third, you describe your product or service as the very best solution available and end the advertisement with a call to action. You tell the prospect to visit your place of business or telephone to set up an appointment or visit your Internet site or take some other action to acquire the product or service immediately. This offers the customer an immediate way to get the solution or benefit he or she now desires.

Here is a simple example: "Drivers have serious car accidents every day when their worn tires give out in fast freeway traffic (problem/pain). Enjoy the peace of mind and security of knowing that you are driving on brand new tires (solution). ABC Tire Company offers you great prices, quick service, and skilled technicians. Come in today at 425 Western Avenue or phone 619 555-5555 (call to action). Don't wait. Do it today. Come in to 425 Western Avenue or phone us to set up an appointment at 619 555-5555. You will be so glad you did."

You don't need to be an advertising genius to write effective copy. You simply have to focus clearly on the most important benefit you offer. Be clear what your product or service does to improve the customer's life or work and tell the customer what action he or she should take immediately to acquire your product or service.

Direct Response Advertising

All advertising for your business must be treated as "direct response advertising." This means that your advertising triggers immediate responses from prospective customers. It translates into immediate sales—today. Creative advertising sells! Period. Effective advertising sells. Period. If your advertising doesn't trigger immediate responses, discontinue it immediately.

The easiest way to test your advertising is to run it up the flagpole and see if anyone salutes. The easiest way to measure the success of your advertisement is that you attract immediate responses that convert into customers who buy more of your product or service and yield you more profits than the cost of the advertising.

Practice Makes Perfect

If you keep testing and measuring, practicing trial and error, asking your customers about how they heard about you and what caused them to contact you or visit, you can eventually develop a method or process of advertising that pays for itself every single time. Once you have developed the ability to attract customers profitably, you can advertise more and more and grow your business almost without limit.

One final point about marketing, advertising, sales, and customer service: always remember to tune into the customers' favorite radio station, WII-FM—"What's in it for me?"

In the final analysis, customers are selfish and expedient. They have a thousand choices. They buy a product or service only when they are convinced that it is the ideal choice for them, at this time, at this price, in this location, and that there is nothing better available as an alternative. You should also keep asking, "What's in it for my customer?" (WII-FMC).

The Goal of Marketing

Marketing includes everything you do from the day you start into business, including choosing your name, your products and services, and every other element of the marketing mix, right up to the moment of selling. The purpose of marketing is to make selling unnecessary. If your marketing efforts were totally effective, your prospective customer would walk through the door, money in hand, ready to buy immediately.

> If your marketing efforts were totally effective, your prospective customer would walk through the door, money in hand, ready to buy immediately.

Unfortunately, this seldom happens. The very best that marketing can usually hope to achieve is excellent lead generation. Good marketing can bring qualified prospects to your door, your telephone, or your Internet site, but from that point on, you now have to convert that lead into a sale and get paid for that sale.

The Selling Process

Selling can be defined as everything that happens from the first contact with the prospective customer all the way through to the satisfactory delivery of the product or service.

If your advertising is effective, it will attract prospective customers to your business. If you are engaged in direct selling, where you telephone and make appointments and then go and see customers personally, you have to prospect for customers. Each part of the professional selling process must take place, no matter how you meet customers for the first time.

1. Prospecting. The first rule of selling is to "spend more time with better prospects." Your first job in the prospecting process is to separate "prospects" from "suspects." Your goal in the initial stages of your first meeting is to determine whether the person is a genuine prospect or just a "tire kicker."

For many people, shopping around is a form of entertainment. They are polite and pleasant and they ask lots of questions, but they have no real intention of buying in the foreseeable future.

In prospecting, you ask carefully planned questions to determine whether this person has a genuine need that your product or service can satisfy. These questions will differ, depending upon what you sell and who you sell it to.

One of the best investments you will ever make is in books, CDs, and professional sales training programs that teach you how to become excellent at prospecting and finding new customers.

2. Establishing Rapport and Trust. Customers today are pampered, spoiled, and fickle. They will only buy from someone they like and who they feel likes them. *"They don't care how much you know until they know how much you care."*

People decide emotionally and then justify logically. In the first few moments with a prospect, you must slow down and take the time to build a minimum level of trust and likeability with that person. You do this by asking friendly questions and listening closely to the answer. You establish rapport and trust by being genuinely interested in the other person, as a person, rather than just as a customer.

3. Identifying Needs. In this part of the sales process, you ask the prospect questions about what he or she is currently doing, what he or she needs at the moment, and what his or her plans are for the future.

Whenever someone asks me for my advice about which one of my programs to buy, I always ask, "What sort of work are you doing now?"

When someone comes into your place of business, perhaps the worst question you can ask is "Can I help you?"

This question will almost always generate the response, "No, thank you, I'm just looking," and the person will soon leave your place of business.

A better opening question would be "Is there anything specific that I can help you with today?"

You could also say, "Thank you for coming in," and then ask, "How can I be of service to you?"

In medicine, they say, "Prescription without examination and diagnosis is malpractice."

Most salespeople unfortunately commit "sales malpractice" every single day. They start talking to the customer about the product or service before they have taken the time to do the examination and the diagnosis.

4. The Presentation. Once you have established rapport with the prospect and clearly identified what he or she wants, needs, and is looking for, you then show how your product or service is the very best choice for this prospect, at this time, all things considered.

You use what is called "educational selling." Instead of trying to persuade the prospect to buy your product, you teach the prospect about your product, what it is made of, how it works, and—especially—what it does for the customer. You teach the special benefits that owning this product offers to the customer. You do not try to sell at all. Instead, you focus on giving the prospect good information and let him or her evaluate that information without pressure.

> Instead of trying to persuade the prospect to buy your product, you teach the prospect about your product, what it is made of,

5. Answering Objections. There are no sales without questions or concerns. A good customer will want to know about what will happen if he or she buys what you are selling. The customer may have questions or concerns about the price, competitive offerings, or the suitability for him or her at this time. You must be prepared to answer these concerns openly and honestly.

6. Closing the Sale. This is often the most stressful part of the sale for both the customer and the salesperson. However, it does not need to be difficult. It simply requires that you develop two or three simple ways of asking the customer to make a buying decision.

   a. The Assumption Close. After your presentation, you ask a question like "Do you like what I've shown you so far?" or "How do you like this?"

   If the customer says something like "It looks pretty good" or "It looks fine," you *assume* the sale and behave exactly as if the customer has said, "Yes, I'll take it."

You ask, "Well, then, would you like me to wrap this up for you?" or "Well, then, if you have no further questions, how soon do you need this?"

b. The Invitational Close. You ask, "Do you have any questions or concerns that I haven't covered?"

When the customer says, "No," you close the sale by saying, "Well, then, why don't you give it a try?" If you are selling services, you say, "Well, then, why don't you give *us* a try?" If you are selling a tangible product, you can ask, "Well, then, why don't you take it?" or "Why don't you buy it?"

In every case, once you have explained your product or service to the customer and explained how he or she can best use it, you should invite him or her to make a buying decision—"Why don't you give it a try?"

c. The Alternative Close. Customers often find it easier to buy if you give them a choice rather than an ultimatum. For example, "Which of these do you prefer, the red one or the blue one?" or "Which do you like better, the Model 25 or the Model 30?"

If you only have a single product, offer a choice between methods of payment: "How would you like to pay for this, cash or charge?" Or you could offer a difference in delivery: "Would you like to take this with you or should we send it out to you tomorrow?"

There are more than 100 ways to close sales of different kinds. In my experience, having trained more than a million salespeople, I have concluded that you only need to know about seven closing techniques. Once you have learned and memorized these techniques, you will have them in your head to use at the appropriate time.

7. Getting Resales and Referrals. Immediately after making a sale, you could ask, "Would you happen to know anyone else who might be interested in getting what you have just purchased?"

To get resales, you must be sure to follow up the sale with excellent customer service, as we will talk about below.

The Most Profitable Sales

The reason that resales and referrals are so important is because they are the most profitable and easiest sales you can make. A sale to a satisfied customer is ten times easier than going out, advertising and selling, and getting a new customer. This means that it takes one tenth of the time, cost, and energy to make a resale as it does to make a first-time sale. All successful, profitable businesses are built on the second sale (and the third, and the fourth, and the fifth, etc.).

A referral from a satisfied customer is 15 times easier to sell to than a cold call or a new customer. This means that it takes 15 times the cost and energy to find a new customer through advertising, promotion, and sales efforts as it does to sell to someone who has been referred to you by a happy customer.

Credibility Is the Key to the Sale

Perhaps the most important word in business success is "credibility." The higher your credibility, the easier it is for someone to buy from you. And everything that you do in your interaction with the customer raises or lowers your credibility. Everything counts.

When you get a referral from a satisfied customer, it will almost invariably be to a friend, relative, or close business associate of the customer. The customer has already established a high level of trust and credibility with that person. When you call on a referral, it is with all the credibility that has already been established by your customer.

> When you call on a referral, it is with all the credibility that has already been established by your customer.

all the credibility that has already been established by your customer. As much as 95 percent of the sale has already been made.

Consistent Customer Service

The third part of successful business development on the way to wealth, after marketing (lead generation) and selling (lead conversion), is customer service and customer satisfaction. As mentioned above, almost any company can attract a customer for the first time. But it is your ability to keep that customer coming back and buying again that is the true measure of your effectiveness as a businessperson.

What customers want more than anything else is for you to fulfill your promises. When they bought from you and gave you money, you made them certain promises about your product or service. These promises may have been written down, spoken, or merely implied in the transaction. But it is only when you fulfill your promises and the customer feels that he or actually got what he or she paid for that the customer will buy from you again and recommend you to friends, relatives, and associates.

Four Levels of Customer Service

There are four levels of customer service. Wherever you are on one of these levels largely determines business success or failure.

1. You meet expectations. The first level is the basic level, the minimum requirement for survival. Without meeting customer expectations consistently, you have no chance in competitive business.

Most anger and other negative emotions in life and in business arise as the result of "frustrated expectations." When you expect to get something, whether or not your expectation is based on fact or fantasy, and your expectation is not fulfilled, you become angry. If someone promises to meet you at a certain time and you wait around for an hour but the person never comes, you will be angry about the situation. Your expectation was frustrated and you were disappointed.

Similarly, customers expect to get certain things when they buy a product or service. They expect that the product or service will work the way you say it will work. They expect that you will treat them politely and courteously. They expect that your billing and payment procedures will be accurate. They expect correct change from you if they are giving you money. They expect that the product will be clean and presentable. They expect that, if they have a question, someone will answer the phone and give them a complete and accurate answer, in a positive and polite tone of voice.

Some customer expectations are *explicit*; they are clear and part of your offering. Other customer expectations are *implicit*, like the expectation that you will treat them politely. They are neither spoken about nor written down, but they exist nonetheless. Your failure to meet customer expectations of either kind will cause customer "blowback" and can frustrate any of your desires for repeat business.

2. You exceed expectations. This is where you do something in the sale, or after the sale, that exceeds what the customer expected. The action of exceeding expectations brings a smile to the customer's face. It causes the customer to feel warm and positive toward you. It makes the customer happy.

All business growth and success in a competitive economy requires that you continually exceed the expectations, both implicit and explicit, of your customers. This of course requires that you are clear about what your customers expect, so that you can go beyond it.

There is a restaurant not far from where I live. This restaurant is always full and has been full for 15 years, ever since it opened. There are many other restaurants that offer food of a similar quality, but this restaurant is always full. Why?

Here's one reason. From the first month that they were open, the manager of the restaurant would make random phone calls to people who had dined at the restaurant. When you phoned in to make a reservation, you gave your name and your phone number. Within a couple of days after your visit, the manager would phone and ask, "How was everything during your visit?"

No other restaurant that I have ever been to has ever used this strategy. It is quite endearing. In most cases, my comments have been positive and uplifting. Occasionally, I've had a problem with a particular dish. The next time I came in, they would always give me a complimentary hors d'oeuvre, dessert, or even a bottle of wine. They would explain that this was to thank me for giving them my candid comments to help them to be better in the future.

People who go to this restaurant are very loyal. They return over and over again. They bring their friends and family members, who also become regular patrons. As I said, the restaurant is always full because they exceed expectations, even in the small effort of phoning their customers afterwards to ask for their opinions.

3. You delight your customers. This is where you do something that is above and beyond the actions of exceeding expectations. You delight your customers when you "go the extra mile." You do something that is considerably more than what they could imagine that the business would do. It comes as a pleasant surprise.

For example, when a woman shops at Nordstrom stores and feels torn among three dresses or outfits, the salesperson will quite cheerfully recommend that she buy all three, take them home, get an opinion from her husband, and then just bring back the ones that she doesn't like.

Nordstrom has a 100 percent refund guarantee policy—no questions asked. You can buy anything from a Nordstrom store, anywhere, and take it back anytime and get a full refund, with no questions and no hassles. For this reason, among others, people who go to Nordstrom stores buy with both hands. Nordstrom consistently delights its customers by making shopping so easy and enjoyable.

4. You amaze your customers. This is when you do something that is so beyond imagination that your customers light up like an electrified Christmas tree and become so excited and impressed that they tell everybody that they know.

Federal Express has a slogan, "When it absolutely, positively has to be there overnight." For this reason, people who absolutely have to get a letter or package delivered use Federal Express to the tune of $50 billion each year.

Some time ago, a blizzard closed the mountain passes between Denver and Breckenridge, Colorado. Federal Express had committed to delivering a rush package to a business in Breckenridge. On his own initiative, the manager of the local Federal Express office chartered a helicopter, at a cost of $7,500, to fly over the mountain, land in the parking lot, and deliver the package.

When the business owner expressed his amazement and delight, the Federal Express manager said, "We value keeping our delivery promises more than the money." He then flew back to Denver. This story has now been repeated thousands of times. It has generated millions and even billions of dollars worth of additional business for FedEx.

When you make a special effort to amaze your customers, by doing something that they could not imagine that a "normal" company would do, you create goodwill and customer loyalty that can generate business year after year.

Stew Leonard, who built the Stew Leonard Dairy Store in Norwalk, Connecticut into the most successful grocery operation in the world, did it all on the basis of incredible customer service.

On a huge rock outside the store, he had engraved the Stew Leonard customer service principle, which I paraphrased earlier: "Rule 1. The customer is always right! Rule 2. If the customer is ever wrong, reread rule 1."

Leonard had a moment of awakening early in his career. By conducting customer surveys, he estimated that a loyal customer who shopped at his supermarket would spend $100 per visit and would visit 50 times each year. He also discovered that the average customer would shop with his store for about 10 years if he or she was satisfied. Doing a quick calculation ($100 x 50 x 10 = $50,000), he concluded that each person who came to his store was a $50,000 customer.

From that moment on, every person who worked in his store, at every job, was trained to imagine a label on the forehead of every customer that read, "$50,000." Each customer was treated as though he or she was there to buy $50,000 worth of groceries. Each customer was treated as though he or she was an extraordinarily valuable customer. And it paid off.

Stew Leonard's carries only 2,000 items. But it sells more of those 2,000 items individually than any other store in the world. And people keep coming, year after year, to experience the fantastic customer service and to bring their friends along for the visit.

The Ultimate Question

Fred Reichheld of Bain & Company wrote a book in 2006 called *The Ultimate Question*. He and his colleagues did many years of market research, interviewing customers in a variety of ways to determine methods to increase customer satisfaction.

After several years of research with many thousands of customers, he concluded that the most important question, the one question that distilled all the other answers to all the other surveys, was *"Would you recommend us to others?"*

> The one question that distilled all the other answers to all the other surveys, was *"Would you recommend us to others?"*

In the final analysis, the true measure of the success of a business, the true evaluation of the products and services sold, is summarized in the answer to that question. "Would you recommend us to others?"

They then instituted a one-to-ten survey. They would ask customers, "On a scale of one to ten, how strongly do you feel about recommending us to others?"

What Reichheld and his associates discovered was that 85 percent of their new business came from people who answered this question with a nine or ten on the scale.

They call this "The Ultimate Question." I think it is one of the greatest breakthroughs ever made in understanding business, marketing, and customer service. This ultimate question can become your focal point and measure for all of your business operations and, especially, all of your interactions with customers. Your goal is for every customer to rank you at a nine or a ten in answering the question, "Would you recommend us to others?"

Moments of Truth

In 1981, Jan Carlzon took over the presidency of troubled Scandinavian Airlines System (SAS). The company had a bad reputation for quality and customer service. It was losing money. Carlzon was brought in to save the airline.

He took the corporate pyramid, with the president on top and the staff at the bottom, and turned it upside down. He announced to the company that, from that day forward, the frontline people, those who dealt with customers, both personally and on the telephone, were at the top of the pyramid and the president, executives, and everyone else in the company worked for them. Everyone in the company, including himself, was lower down in the corporate pyramid than the people who worked with customers.

Carlzon then called every customer contact a "moment of truth" (a term coined by Richard Normann in his book, *Service Management*). He said that every single time a customer comes into contact with anybody in SAS, it is a moment of truth that determines whether they use SAS or a competitor in the future.

Every person in the company was empowered to do everything possible to make every customer contact a positive "moment of truth." Their job was not only to meet expectations, but to exceed expectations and to amaze and delight customers in every way possible.

By implementing this philosophy companywide, the people of Scandinavian Airline System turned the business around. It went from losing money to becoming highly profitable. It went from being criticized by customers to being one of the most desirable airlines in Europe. By focusing on customer service, on ensuring a high score to the ultimate question, "Would you recommend us to others?" Carlzon and his people created a modern marketing miracle.

The Importance of Systems

The customer is the most important person in your business. Without customers, there is no business. To grow your business, you need more and better customers. You need to attract people to buy from you and to bring their friends. You need to upsell and cross-sell those customers so that they buy more each time and they buy more frequently. In every case it is customers, customers, customers.

> To ensure a high, steady, and increasing number of customers, you must continually test and measure every part of your marketing mix.

To ensure a high, steady, and increasing number of customers, you must continually test and measure every part of your marketing mix. You must continually evaluate your business against the four keys to marketing strategy. You must continually improve in every area and activity of your sales process. One small change can dramatically improve the results and profitability of your business.

Your Customer Service Policy

In order to market, advertise, and sell effectively, you need to create systems that enable you to measure the effectiveness of everything you do. You need systems that spell out exactly what each person will do at each customer contact. You need written scripts so that everyone who answers the phone says exactly the same thing. You need detailed plans so that every customer is treated in a warm, courteous, and professional fashion. You need systems at every part of the business to ensure that every customer experience with you is excellent in every way.

You need a customer service policy that spells out, on paper, exactly how customers will be treated under every circumstance. Your goal is to create the "ultimate customer experience" in every interaction. Your goal with your customer service system is to ensure that people are delighted and amazed with their experience in dealing with you and your business.

Become Brilliant on the Basics

Success in business is both simple and difficult. It is simple in that it consists of offering customers a product or service that they want, need, and are willing to pay for. It is simple in that all customers really ask is to be treated in a warm, friendly, and courteous manner, just as you would like to be treated if you were a customer. It is simple in that you give customers the services that they expect and then constantly strive to exceed those expectations.

Selling is difficult and complicated because we are working in a fast-changing, competitive world. Whatever you do today that works will soon be copied by your competitor. Whatever you do today that is working will soon become obsolete and will have to be replaced by something better, faster, and cheaper.

The good news is that you have all the talent and ability that you need to build and operate a successful business. You have all the intelligence and creativity you require to attract prospects, to convert those prospects into happy customers, and then to service those customers in such a way that they come back over and over again and bring their friends.

103

By dedicating yourself to continuous and never-ending improvement in each of these areas, you virtually guarantee a healthy, growing, and prosperous business. You will stride confidently down the way to wealth.

Action Exercises

1. Resolve to spend 50 percent or more of your time on customer acquisition from now on. Make it a central focus of everyone in your business.

2. Determine how much you are spending to "buy customers" and how much you can afford to spend.

3. Test and measure every advertisement and method of promotion to be sure that it is "free" in that it pays for itself in additional profits.

4. Analyze your selling process and be sure that everyone who deals with every lead or customer is thoroughly trained to convert as many leads as possible.

5. Create a customer service policy and be sure that everyone in your company knows exactly what to do and say in every customer contact.

6. Identify your most important competitive advantage, your "unique selling proposition," and build all your advertising, promotion, and selling efforts around it.

7. Determine what you will have to do to get your customers to give you a nine or ten score on the question, "Based on your experience with us, would you recommend us to your friends and family?"

CHAPTER FIVE

Selling Your Way to the Top

The toughest thing about the power of trust is that it's very difficult to build and easy to destroy. The essence of trust building is to emphasize the similarities between you and the customer.

—Thomas J. Watson, Sr.

 ROM THE DAY YOU START YOUR BUSINESS UNTIL THE DAY YOU retire, you are in sales of some kind. Whatever your title, you are a "salesperson." You are selling your products or services, selling banks on loaning you money, selling suppliers on giving you credit and good prices, and selling people on the idea of working for you rather than for someone else. The only question is "How good are you at selling?"

Have you ever wondered why some salespeople are more successful than others? Have you ever wondered why some salespeople make more money, live in nicer homes, drive newer cars, and dine in better restaurants? Have you ever asked why some people rise to the top of the sales profession in a few months or years and earn the respect and esteem of the important people around them? Have you ever wanted to achieve the same results?

Welcome to the crowd! Everyone wants to be successful. Everyone wants to have a nice life with a great family, a good income, a nice car, and a wonderful future. In the coming pages, you will discover how you can become one of the most productive, best-selling, and highest-paid salespeople in your profession. You will learn the secrets of success practiced by the happiest and highest-paid sales professionals in every field. You will learn how to run circles around your competitors and become one of the most respected people in your industry.

> The good news is that you have the potential, right now, with your current talents and abilities, to be far, far better than you've ever been before.

The good news is that you have the potential, right now, with your current talents and abilities, to be far, far better than you've ever been before. Anything anyone else has done, you can do as well—if you want it badly enough and if you are willing to work at it long enough.

Time to Get Serious

The turning point in your career comes when you finally decide to *get serious*. Many people drift along in selling for years, achieving average levels of performance and enjoying average rewards. But then something happens to them. Sometimes they get excited. Sometimes they get angry. Sometimes they see other people who are doing far better than they are who are certainly no more talented. At that moment, for whatever reason, they make a firm decision that their future is going to be different from their past. They *get serious*.

The turning point toward greater sales in your business is when you finally make the decision to become one of the very best in your field. You resolve to pay any price, to make any effort, to develop any quality or skill, and to overcome any obstacle necessary to move to the top of the profession of selling.

Pay the Price of Preparation

No one becomes excellent at selling by accident. It only happens by design. You first make a decision to excel and then you create a plan. You chart out a course of action. You organize every day, every week, and every month into a part of a continuous process of professional growth and development.

As Paul "Bear" Bryant, the famous University of Alabama football coach, once said, *"It's not the will to win that counts. Virtually everybody wants to be a winner. It's the will to prepare to win that makes champions."*

To become excellent in selling, you must make a firm, unequivocal decision to be *the best* at what you do. You must decide to join the top 10 percent of people in volume of sales. You must set superb performance as your overarching goal and you never give up until you achieve it.

Remember: everyone who is in the top 10 percent of selling today was once in the bottom 10 percent. Everyone who is ahead in this profession was once behind. Everyone who is at the front of the line started at the back of the line.

What Others Have Done, You Can Do

Abraham Lincoln once said, *"The fact that some succeed greatly is evidence that others may succeed greatly as well."*

The Law of Cause and Effect says, "for every effect in your life, there is a specific cause."

If you can identify the effects that you want—higher sales, higher income, greater profitability, more success, respect and esteem from others, you can then trace back and find out what other successful people who started at the bottom did to achieve those goals. When you do the same things that other successful people do, over and over, you will eventually get the same results.

The Law of Incremental Improvement lies at the root of all great success in life. This law says that every great achievement is an accumulation of hundreds and even thousands of tiny efforts that no one ever sees or appreciates. But the accumulation of these efforts, day after day, week after week, and month after month adds up to an extraordinary career and an extraordinary life.

The poet Henry Wordsworth Longfellow once wrote:

"The heights by great men reached and kept
Were not attained by sudden flight.
But they while their companions slept
Were toiling upward in the night."

Mastery Requires Long, Hard Work

Here is a great rule for achieving personal excellence: *"Anything worth doing well is worth doing poorly at first—and often it's worth doing poorly several times until you master it."*

When you learn a new method or technique in selling, resolve to try it out five or ten times before you pass judgment on it. Invariably, the first time you try something new, you will do it poorly. One of the primary reasons for failure and underachievement is that when people do something poorly the first time out and it doesn't work, they quit, they give up. As a result, they don't improve and make little or no progress at all.

> When you learn a new method or technique in selling, resolve to try it out five or ten times before you pass judgment on it.

But this is not for you. You have made a decision to become excellent at selling. You know that anything that anyone else has done you can do as well. You know that there are no limits on what you can accomplish except the limits you place on your own mind.

You also know that you can learn anything you need to learn to achieve any goal that you can set for yourself. You know that anything that anyone else has learned and practiced you can learn and practice as well until you master it.

Commit to Excellence

Commit today to read every book that can help you in your field. Listen to audio programs in your car as you drive from place to place. Take all the training you can get, both the training available through your company and other training offered by companies that specialize in training salespeople. Never stop learning and improving.

Your decision to become absolutely excellent in selling will have a greater effect on the revenues of your business and your profitability than perhaps any other decision you make.

The fact is that you will be happy and successful in your business only when you absolutely know, deep down inside, that you can sell well in any market. And this is completely up to you.

Take Charge of Your Sales Results

When you start a business, you take complete charge of your financial destiny. You become *unemployable* to any other company. From that day onward, the biggest mistake you can make is to think that you work for anyone else but yourself.

From the time you start your first business until the time you retire, you are self-employed. You are the president of your own company. You are the architect of your own destiny and the master of your own fate.

This attitude of self-employment shows in the acceptance of a high level of *personal responsibility* for every area of your life. It is the core quality of high performance and personal effectiveness. The attitude of self-employment is the foundation of self-reliance and personal power.

> The attitude of self-employment is the foundation of self-reliance and personal power.

As the president of your own company, you are completely responsible for every aspect of your business. You are in complete charge of marketing and selling, production, distribution, quality control, and customer satisfaction. You are responsible for training and development, for upgrading the skills and abilities of yourself and your staff.

You Control Your Own Income

You are paid in direct proportion to your performance and your results. You are totally responsible for your output and your contribution. You determine your own income and design your own future—every single day.

Superior people in every field accept complete responsibility for their lives and their work. They refuse to make excuses or to blame other people for their problems. They believe that, as President Harry Truman once said, "The buck stops here."

The best salespeople in every field seem to have feelings of high self-esteem, self-reliance, and self-responsibility. They see themselves as being completely in charge of their own lives. They never complain, never explain. If there is something in their lives that they don't like, they work to change it.

Top businesspeople know that they are where they are and what they are because of themselves. You are where you are today as the result of all your past choices and decisions. If there is any part of your life that you are not satisfied with, you are always free to make new and better choices and decisions.

Become a Master of Change

Resolve today to be a *master* of change rather than a *victim* of change. Decide to be a *creator* of circumstances rather than a *creature* of circumstances. Decide today to take complete charge of your life and your sales. Be proactive rather than reactive. Your attitude of self-responsibility, of seeing yourself as completely in charge of sales results, will do more to give you the feelings of self-confidence and personal power than perhaps any other decision you can make. Say to yourself throughout the day, "I am responsible! I am responsible!"

Committing to excellence in selling, to becoming one of the very best salespeople in your field, combined with the attitude of self-responsibility, will make you *unstoppable* in your business. Becoming excellent at selling will guarantee your success.

Develop the Winning Edge in Selling

One of the greatest business principles discovered in the 20th century is the "Winning Edge Concept." This concept says that *"Small differences in ability can translate into large differences in results."*

The best salespeople have developed small "winning edges" that translate into huge differences in sales results. This is why the top 20 percent of salespeople make 80 percent of the sales and, on average, earn ten and 15 times as much as those in the bottom 80 percent.

This 80/20 rule applies to selling in another way. Fully 80 percent of sales success is *psychological*. Only 20 percent is technical. Only 20 percent is contained in all the product knowledge and specific sales skills that you can learn. Fully 80 percent of your sales and your income will be determined by your attitude and your personality.

Think like a Winner

The highest-paid salespeople have certain attitudes and qualities of thinking in common. When you begin to think like the top salespeople and develop the same attitudes as they have, you will soon be making more sales, more easily than ever. You will soon be generating the same high levels of profitability as the top people.

Millions of dollars have been spent and thousands of salespeople have been tested to uncover the qualities that would best predict high levels of success in selling. Dr. Martin Seligman of the University of Pennsylvania, who conducted these studies for 22 years, finally concluded that the very highest-paid salespeople are far more optimistic than the average salesperson.

> The quality of *optimism*, having a positive mental attitude, is a more accurate predictor of success than any other single measure.

The quality of *optimism*, having a positive mental attitude, is a more accurate predictor of success than any other single measure. Optimism means that you have a generally positive and constructive attitude toward your life and work.

Develop a Positive Mental Attitude

A positive mental attitude has been defined as "a positive response to stress."

Anyone can be positive and optimistic when things are going well. It is only when you face the inevitable ups and downs of rejection and disappointment that you demonstrate what you are really made of.

Epictetus, the Greek philosopher, said, "Circumstances do not *make* the man. They merely reveal him to himself."

There are three qualities that lead to a positive mental attitude. Each of these qualities is learnable. Each of these qualities is demonstrated by the highest-paid salespeople in every profession. Each of these qualities can be acquired by practice and repetition.

Stay Hungry

First of all, top salespeople are *ambitious*. They are hungry. They really want to be successful. They see themselves as capable of being the best in their field. They are determined to get into the top 20 percent of their professions and then into the top 10 percent. They know that anything that anyone else has done they can do as well.

Top salespeople believe that they *deserve* to be the best and to enjoy the rewards that go with sales success. The word *deserve* comes from two Latin words meaning "from service." They know that they fully deserve anything that they can attain from serving others, from helping their customers to acquire products and services that can improve their lives and work.

Top salespeople see their ability to sell and their sales results as stepping stones to higher achievement and to financial success. Consequently, they set high standards for themselves. They are determined to get better and better and to sell more and more.

Do the Thing You Fear

The second attitude or quality that leads to optimism and sales success is courage: top salespeople are *courageous*. They work continually to confront the fears, especially the fears of failure and rejection that hold most people back.

Vincent Van Gogh said, "The key to success is for you to *make a habit throughout your life of doing the things you fear.*" Ralph Waldo Emerson wrote, "Make a habit throughout your life of doing the things you fear. If you do the thing you fear, the death of fear is certain."

The average person evades and avoids the things that he or she fears. The superior salesperson, on the other hand, turns toward the fear and confronts it.

Are you afraid of prospecting? Then force yourself to prospect, by telephone and personally, over and over again, until the fear eventually disappears.

The *primary* reason that salespeople underachieve and fail is the fear of rejection, the fear of calling on strangers. You can overcome this fear by realizing that rejection is not personal.

No one can reject you as a person. They can merely reject your initial approach with a new product or service. No one knows *you* well enough to reject you as an individual.

The Greek philosopher, Aristotle, once said, "The way to develop a quality, if you have it not, is to act on every occasion where the quality is required as if you had it already."

The way to become fearless in your selling activities is to act in every respect as if you were fearless already. The more courageous and confident you become, the more optimistic you will be and the more positive your attitude will be.

Make a Total Commitment

The third attitude or quality of top salespeople is *commitment*. Top salespeople are totally committed to their companies, to their products and services, to their customers—and to themselves. They make a 100-percent, wholehearted commitment to doing what they do and doing it well.

Perhaps the most important word in selling is the word "caring." Customers today are more sophisticated and demanding than ever and they will buy only from someone who they feel really *cares* about them and their situation.

The more committed you are to what you are selling, the more you care about other people. The more you care about them and how your product or service can help to improve their lives or work, the easier it becomes for you to sell.

Caring translates into enthusiasm. And selling has often been called a "transfer of enthusiasm." When the enthusiasm you feel for the goodness of what you sell transfers to your customer, the sale is complete.

> When the enthusiasm you feel for the goodness of what you sell transfers to your customer, the sale is complete.

You never see top salespeople who merely dabble in their professions. They are totally committed to the importance and value of what they do. They start a little earlier, work a little harder, and stay a little later. They learn their product and service information inside and out. And when they sell, they sell wholeheartedly so that their customers experience their confidence and enthusiasm and are moved more readily to buying.

Be the Best in Selling

Join the "winner's circle" in selling. Develop the "winning edges" in your profession. Especially develop the attitude and personality of the happiest, highest-performing people in your field.

Be positive, optimistic, and confident. Be *ambitious* for yourself and your business; set high standards for what you can accomplish.

Develop the quality of *courage* by acting, in every situation where you might feel nervous or unsure, as if it were impossible to fail. As Emerson advised, do the thing you fear and the death of fear is certain.

> **D**evelop the quality of *courage* by acting, in every situation where you might feel nervous or unsure, as if it were impossible to fail.

Commit yourself wholeheartedly to your profession, to being the very best and to doing the very best job possible. Make it clear to your customers that you really care about helping them to improve their lives and work.

Change with the Times

Selling has changed dramatically in the last few years and you have to change as well if you want to maximize your sales.

In the 1950s and 1960s, customers were relatively unsophisticated. The selection of products and services was limited. The salesperson was more knowledgeable than the customer. As a result, the entire emphasis in selling was on the sales approach and sales methodology, on talking people into buying.

Sales were based on the AIDA model—*attention, interest, desire, action.* The salesperson said something to get the customer's *attention*, aroused *interest* by explaining features, aroused *desire* by explaining benefits, and then called for *action* and closed the sale.

By the 1970s, customers had become far more knowledgeable, sophisticated, experienced, and demanding. The requirements for effective selling shifted from the old model to the new model of selling. The key to understanding the new model of selling is realizing that relationships are more important now than anything else in professional selling.

Relationships Are Everything

There are four parts to the new model of selling.

The first part, which determines fully 40 percent of the sales transaction, is to develop a high-trust relationship between yourself and the prospective customer. Trust is the glue that holds sales relationships together. Trust is the foundation of your relationships with your customers, the foundation that you must build before you can make any attempt to sell your product or service.

The second part of the new model of selling, fully 30 percent of the sales process, is accurately identifying the customer's real needs relative to what you are selling or the customer's real problems that your product or service can solve.

The way you develop trust is by asking questions related to the customer's needs and then by listening attentively to the answers. The more you ask questions and listen carefully, the more the customer trusts you. The more the customer trusts you, the more the customer will open up and expand on his or her real needs, wants, and desires.

The great rule for success in selling today is "listening builds trust." When you listen attentively, without interrupting, your customer feels more important and valuable. His or her self-esteem increases. Your customer likes you better and is more open to doing business with you.

If the customer likes you, the details won't get in the way. But if the customer doesn't like you, the details will trip you up every step of the way.

The third part of the new model of selling, 20 percent of the process, is the *presentation*. However, in the professional presentation, you focus exclusively on showing the customer that his or her needs can be met or his or her problems can be solved with the unique features and benefits of the product or service that you are selling. Your presentation is not "canned." It is carefully crafted and tailored to respond specifically to what your customer has told you during the initial stages of the conversation.

The final part of the new model of selling is the confirmation or *closing* phase. This is a relatively small part of the sale, the final 10 percent. If you have built trust, clarified needs, and presented well in the first parts of the sale, this is the natural conclusion of the sales process.

In selling today, relationships are everything. The more and better relationships you can establish, with more and better customers, the more sales you will make and the more profitable your business will be.

Approach each new customer as if you will be selling to this customer for many years to come. Focus all your attention on developing a high-quality, high-trust relationship. When you build and maintain this type of relationship, the sale will happen by itself. And the sales will go on, year after year.

Get into Your Customer's Head

Positioning is everything. The way you are positioned or perceived in the heart and mind of your customer will determine everything that your customer does in relationship to you and your product or service recommendations.

For the customer, *perception is reality*. It is not who you *really* are or what your product or service *really* is; it is how your customer thinks and feels about you that determines whether or not your customer buys and continues to buy.

For this reason, the very best salespeople position themselves as *consultants* with their customers, rather than as salespeople. They think of themselves as consultants and they act like consultants in everything they do and say.

Here is an important rule: people accept you at your own evaluation of yourself.

How do you position yourself as a consultant in the account? Simply tell the customer, "I see myself more as a consultant than as a salesperson." The customer will see you as you see yourself.

Act Like a Consultant

How can you tell who a person *really* is? Only by looking at their actions, at what they *do*. You are evaluated by others on the basis of your behavior. If you act like a consultant, people will accept that you are a consultant, even if they began by thinking you were a salesperson.

When you think of the words that people use to describe a consultant, you think of the following: *"expert, knowledgeable, objective, friend, problem-solver, counselor, advisor, good questioner, helper, teacher, and good listener."*

To partner with your customers, to position yourself as a consultant and as an advisor, you must simply "act the part." When you meet a customer for the first time, you can open the conversation by saying, *"Mr. Customer, thank you for your time. I want you to know that I am not here to sell you anything. I see myself more as a consultant and in our time together today what I would like to do is to ask you a few questions to see if there isn't some way that we can help you achieve your goals in a cost-effective manner."*

From that moment onward, you behave as a consultant would behave. Instead of talking and waving prices lists and brochures, you ask good questions, listen intently to the answers, and look for a problem or need that your product or service can solve or satisfy for the customer.

As a consultant, a partner, you position yourself with the customer by using inclusive words such as "we" and "our." For example, you say, "What we seem to have here is a problem in this particular area," or "Our goal in this area should be to achieve this particular objective."

Salespeople sell *at* the customer while consultants sell *with* the customer. At the end of your question-and-answer sequence, when it is clear to both of you that your product or service can be helpful to the customer, you do not "close the sale." Instead, you make *recommendations* for action: "Mr. Customer, based on what we have discussed, what I would recommend for you would be the following."

> Salespeople sell *at* the customer while consultants sell *with* the customer.

When your customers view you as a consultant, as a partner, as a friend who is helping them to improve their lives and work, they will buy from you over and over again and recommend you to others.

All the highest-paid salespeople, in every field, are perceived as consultants and partners by their customers. When you achieve this positioning in the minds and hearts of your customers, you will sell far more than with any other approach.

Sell Strategically

Average salespeople throw themselves at the customer like dogs chasing a passing car. Top salespeople, in contrast, think strategically, plan strategically, and act strategically in everything they do. As a result they make five and ten times as many sales and vastly more money than average salespeople.

You start selling strategically by standing back and looking at the *big picture*. Begin with your territory. What is your market? Where is your market? Who exactly are the potential customers within your territory and your market area? Take time to think before acting so that every action you take is aimed at generating the maximum result.

As we covered in the last chapter, there are four keys to selling strategically:

- specialization
- differentiation
- segmentation
- concentration

The more and better you think in terms of the "Big Four," the more and better you will sell and the faster you will sell.

Target Each Customer Specifically

Specialization refers to the unique application or use of your product or service. What has it been designed to do for your customer? Remember: customers do not buy products or services; they buy solutions to their problems, ways to satisfy their desires, and methods to achieve their goals.

Your product or service has been designed to satisfy a specific need, to solve a specific problem, or to achieve a specific goal for your customer. In selling, amateurs talk about *features* while professionals talk about *benefits*. Amateurs talk about what the product *is* while professionals talk about what the product *does* specifically for the customer.

Think through the area of specialization for your product and then think through your specific *individual* areas of specialization. You have personal abilities that make you special, different from other salespeople. How can you best apply your special talents and abilities to selling the special features and benefits of your product or service?

Emphasize Your Superiority

The second part of strategic selling, *differentiation*, is the determinant of the sale. It is the key to great sales success. All top sales professionals are excellent at differentiating their product or service from those of their competitors.

Your ability to differentiate what you sell, to show your customer that your product or service is better, superior, and different in some way from those of all your competitors is the key to more sales at higher prices. If you cannot differentiate what you're selling from what your competitors are selling, you will always have to sell on the basis of price.

What is the "unique selling proposition" of your product or service? If you had to select one specific feature or benefit that makes your product different from and better than any other product on the market today, what would it be?

What is your area of "competitive advantage"? What is your "area of excellence"? What is it that your customers say that your product or service offers that no other product or service offers in exactly the same way?

Your ability to identify your "differential advantage" and then to overwhelmingly convince your prospect that he or she will enjoy this special benefit by buying from you is the key to your success in professional selling.

By the way, one of the ways to differentiate your product or service is through the uniqueness or special nature of your character and personality. No other product or service for sale in the market comes with *you* as part of the package. Be sure you emphasize that when a customer buys from you, he or she gets *you* as part of the deal.

Determine Your Ideal Customers

The third part of strategic selling is *segmentation*. Look over your territory and your market and ask yourself, "Who are the prospects who can most benefit from the special qualities of my product or service and my competitive advantage or area of excellence?"

Ideal prospects are those who are the easiest to sell to, those who can most benefit most rapidly from the special benefits of your product or service. Who are they?

All success in selling today comes from segmentation, from defining those prospects and markets that can most rapidly benefit from the special features, benefits, and qualities that you have to offer.

All customers are not the same. Some customers are more valuable than others. Some customers can make a buying decision far faster and easier than others. This is your chosen customer segment. This is the group of prospective customers that you must identify and pinpoint to be in the top 10 percent of your field.

Focus Your Energies

The fourth key to strategic selling is *concentration*. This refers to your ability to focus your efforts on your highest-probability prospects and to sell to only them.

Remember: all prospects for your product or service are not necessarily *your* prospects. There are some people to whom you can sell much easier than others. For example, if you are inexperienced, you should not be attempting to sell to highly sophisticated buyers in major corporations. You should focus your selling efforts on customers with whom you are more comfortable.

> Remember: all prospects for your product or service are not necessarily *your* prospects.

One of the rules for sales success is to "always sell at your own level." Always sell to the kind of people who are similar to you in attitudes, background, education, experience, and income. As you grow as a professional salesperson, you can raise the level of quality and sophistication of your customers.

With regard to concentration, you should divide your prospects into three groups—"A" prospects, "B" prospects, and "C" prospects. "A" prospects are the top 20 percent of prospects, who can represent fully 80 percent of your sales. "B" prospects are medium prospects, who, if they buy, will be medium customers. The "C" prospects are also important, but they are not as important as "A" or "B" prospects.

Once you have segmented your market, you must dedicate yourself to *spending more time with better prospects.* You must exhaust your population of "A" prospects before you spend time on "B" or "C" prospects. You must discipline yourself to focus your efforts where you have the greatest possibilities of high sales and rewards.

To sell strategically, you must plan every day, every hour in advance. You must plan your weeks the week or weekend before. You must plan your months the month before. You must plan your year like a military strategy, thinking through and determining exactly where and how you will get the sales that will generate the income that you desire for that year.

The more carefully you plan and the better you execute your plans, the more time you will spend with better prospects and the higher and better sales you will achieve. When you sell strategically, you will move into the top 10 percent in your field.

Maximize Your Most Valuable Asset

What is your most valuable asset? An asset can be defined as "something that yields a predictable stream of cash flow over time." Using this definition, what is *your* most valuable asset in your own personal world?

The answer is simple. Your most valuable asset is your "earning ability." It is your ability to generate cash flow by applying your brains and your talents to selling your products and services.

You could lose your house, your car, your bank account, your job, and everything you have. But as long as you keep your earning ability intact, you could walk out tomorrow and begin generating tens of thousands of dollars per year of income by applying your brain power to the opportunities in the marketplace around you.

It is very easy to take your earning ability for granted. But remember: it has taken all of your education, effort, and experience to cultivate and develop your earning ability to the high level that it is at today. You must be constantly aware of the value and importance of this asset and do everything possible over time to maintain and increase its value and potential cash flow.

Use Your Most Precious Resource

What is your most precious resource? Your most precious resource, the one resource in your life that is essential and irreplaceable, is your *time*. If you lose everything but you still have enough time, you can make it all back again.

> Your most precious resource, the one that is essential and irreplaceable, is your *time*.

Your entire life today—materially, emotionally, and physically—is a reflection of how well you have traded your time, your life, over the years. Are you happy with the results of your trading activities? If not, you can begin immediately today to trade your time better, to achieve greater results and rewards in the months and years ahead.

Earlier in this chapter, I mentioned the Law of Incremental Improvement and how important it is to your success. There is a simple formula that you can use to apply this law to dramatically increase your knowledge and skills and to leverage your talents and abilities beyond anything you have ever imagined.

The 1000-Percent Formula

We call this the *1000-Percent Formula*. By following this formula, you can increase your productivity, performance, and output by 1000 percent, or more, over the next ten years.

How does it work? It is simple.

The formula is based on *kaizen*, the Japanese philosophy of "continuous betterment." By improving yourself and your abilities by one tenth of one percent per day, you can increase your overall productivity, performance, and output by one half of one percent in a five-day week. If you become one half of one percent better per week, that will translate into a two-percent improvement every four weeks or a 26-percent improvement over the course of a year.

Question: "Is it possible for you, if you really wanted to, to improve your overall productivity, performance, and output by 26 percent over the next 12 months?" Put another way, "Can you, by reading, learning, and applying new ideas and information, every single day, become one half of one percent better per week over time?" And the answer, based on the experience of thousands of salespeople, is "Of course!"

Could you continue this 26 percent per year improvement year after year, for ten years? And the answer is "Yes"—if you *decide* to.

The results? 26 percent multiplied times ten years, with compounding, means an improvement of approximately 1008 percent. This huge improvement requires only that you become just one tenth of one percent better each day.

So, how do you do it?

Seven Steps to a 1000-Percent Improvement

The 1000-Percent Formula consists of seven steps.

Step one: *Read 30-60 minutes per day* in your field every morning. This reading will translate into approximately one book per week, 50 books per year, and 500 books in ten years.

Reading one hour per day, each morning, in sales or business, will make you one of the most knowledgeable, skilled, and highest-paid professionals in your field in the nation, over time.

Step two: *Rewrite your major goals*, in the present tense, each morning. Use a spiral notebook. By rewriting your goals every morning, you impress them deeper and deeper into your subconscious mind. You activate all your mental powers. You become focused, channeled, concentrated, and highly effective at achieving your goals. This one exercise of rewriting your goals each day can, all by itself, give you a 1000-percent increase over ten years.

Step three: *Plan every day in advance.* The best time is the night before or the weekend before. Think on paper! Always work from a written plan. Organize your activities by priority so that you always have a clear track to run on.

One of the major reasons for underachievement and failure in selling is that "failing to plan is planning to fail." *All* top salespeople work from a written plan and they use a structured time planner to organize every activity of the working day.

Step four: *Always concentrate on the most valuable use of your time.* The primary reason for individual success in America is that top people do more things of higher value. The number-one reason for *failure* in America is that people spend too much time doing things of low value or even no value.

When you discipline yourself to always concentrate on the most valuable use of your time, every minute of every day, you will accomplish more in a few months and years than the average person accomplishes in a lifetime.

Step five: *Listen to educational audio programs* in your car. Turn "driving time" into "learning time." Turn your car into a university on wheels. The average sales professional spends 500-1000 hours each year in his or her car. If you turn this time into high-quality, educational time, you will become one of the smartest, most skilled, and most highly paid sales professionals in the country.

Step six: *Ask two questions after every sales call.*
The first question is "What did I do right?"

Think of everything you did *right* in that sales presentation. This helps you to recall and repeat those things for your next presentation.

The second question is "What would I do differently?"

Do an "instant replay" of your sales call and evaluate it in terms of how you could improve it next time. By thinking of what you did right and what you would do differently, you emphasize the positive and ignore the negative. You set yourself up mentally to repeat the best aspects of your most recent presentation and to be even better in the future.

> **B**y thinking of what you did right and what you would do differently, you emphasize the positive and ignore the negative.

Step seven: *Treat every person you meet like a "million-dollar customer."* Treat everyone you meet as though he or she were the most important person in the world.

Since each person already thinks that he or she is the most important person in the world, when you treat people as if they were, they will like you and appreciate you and want to do business with you more than with anyone else.

You are your most valuable asset. Your time is your most precious resource. And by working on yourself and using your time well to increase your earning ability, you can become one of the most competent, most confident, most skilled, and highest-paid people in your profession.

Double Your Output

The average salesperson in America works only one and one half hours per day—approximately 20 percent of the time. According to a study by Columbia University and corroborated by research from *Sales & Marketing Management* magazine, this statistic hasn't changed in more than 50 years.

The average salesperson makes about two calls per day and spends most of the rest of the time on idle socializing, personal business, paperwork, shuffling business cards, phone calls to friends and family, and travel time.

But not the top salespeople! The top salespeople make every minute count, from morning to night. They develop the personal management skills that virtually guarantee that they will be among the top 10 percent of producers and earners in their fields. And so can you.

Set Clear Goals and Plans

Sales success, in its simplest terms, requires clearly written and executed sales goals, plans, and activities. Clarity is the key. Self-discipline is the guarantee. Think, decide what you need to do, and then discipline yourself to do it, over and over, until you get the results you desire.

Start with your personal income goals. How much do you want to earn over the next 12 months? All top salespeople know exactly what they are going to earn in the coming year. Poor salespeople usually have no idea. They have to wait until they get their W-2 forms at the end of the year to figure out how they did.

Once you have written down your annual sales goal, divide that figure by the number of months, weeks, days, and even hours you intend to work to achieve that goal. For example, if your goal is to earn $50,000 next year, this means that you will have to earn approximately $1,000 per week, $200 per day, and $25 per hour for an eight-hour day.

Discipline Your Time Usage

Here's the rule: once you have decided that you need to earn $25 per hour in order to earn $50,000 per year, refuse to do anything that does not pay $25 per hour. Do not drop off your dry cleaning, pick up your laundry, shuffle your business cards, or make your own photocopies. These activities do not pay $25 per hour.

Ask yourself continually, "Would I pay someone else $25 per hour, out of my own pocket, to do what I am doing right now?"

If the answer is "No!" then slam on your personal brakes, stop engaging in that activity, and start doing the things that can pay you $25 per hour or more. And what are these activities? They are *prospecting, presenting, and closing sales.* When you are selling, you are in the business of creating and keeping customers. You get paid $25 per hour or more for *new business development.* Everything that you do that is not developing new customers and new business is a relative waste of your time.

Determine the Activities Necessary

Once you have determined the amount of money that you want to make per hour, per day, per week, per month, and per year, define your work in terms of the *activities* necessary to achieve that level of income. How many calls will you have to make each day? How many presentations? How many proposals? How many follow-up calls? And ultimately, how many sales?

Here's the key. Activities are *controllable.* Sales are not. You can never tell with complete accuracy where your next sale is coming from. But if you control the activities that go into each sale, you can indirectly control and determine the number of sales you will eventually achieve.

Set Specific Sales Goals

Once you have clear *income goals* for yourself and the coming sales period, you need clear *sales goals* as well. How much of your products and services and which products and services will you have to sell to achieve your income goals? The very best salespeople are absolutely clear about what they have to sell to achieve their overall income targets. You must be clear as well.

129

Set Specific Personal Goals

Perhaps the most important part of striving toward sales success is your *personal* goals. Sales success and a high income are really just means to an end. The reason you want to be successful in your career is

> The highest-achieving salespeople have clear, specific, written goals, time-bound and with both deadlines and sub-deadlines.

because there are so many things that you want to have and enjoy in your life. What are your goals in those areas?

The highest-achieving salespeople have clear, specific, written goals, time-bound and with both deadlines and sub-deadlines. Unsuccessful salespeople have very vague goals, usually just fantasies and wishes that have no energy to drive them forward.

Seven Steps to Goal Achieving

Take the time to plan to achieve your goals, following these seven steps:

- **Step one:** Decide exactly what you want—personally, financially, and in your career.
- **Step two:** Write it down in clear, specific language. Writing makes your goal concrete and tangible.
- **Step three:** Determine the price you are going to have to pay to achieve this goal. What sacrifices will you have to make?
- **Step four:** Set a deadline on your goal. Set sub-deadlines as well.
- **Step five:** Make a plan to achieve your goal. List everything that you will have to do to get from where you are to where you want to go.
- **Step six:** Set priorities on your plan and select the most important thing that you can do immediately to begin bringing your plan to fruition.
- **Step seven:** Take action on the most important activity and then resolve to do something every day that moves you toward your most important goals.

Set Priorities on Your Tasks

The final step to doubling your output is to set priorities and then to concentrate single-mindedly on the most valuable use of your time. Here are some questions that you can use to guide your activities throughout every hour of every day.

1. What are my highest-value activities? What things contribute the greatest value to myself and my company?

2. Why am I on the payroll? What specific, measurable accomplishments have I been hired to do for my company?

3. What are my key result areas? What are the things that I absolutely, positively must do well to be excellent at my job?

4. What one skill, if I developed it and applied it appropriately, would have the greatest positive impact on my career? Where and how can I begin developing this skill?

5. What can I, and only I, do that, if I do it well, will make a real difference to me and my career? There is usually only one answer to this question at any given time.

6. Is what I am doing right now leading to a sale? (If it's not, stop doing it and start doing something that is the answer to this question.)

7. What is the most valuable use of my time right now? (This is the key question that will guarantee you extraordinary success in your sales career.)

Your ability to set goals, make plans, establish priorities, and concentrate single-mindedly on the most important thing that you could possibly be doing will absolutely guarantee that you will be one of the most respected, most productive, and highest-paid people in sales.

Action Exercises

1. List three reasons why a prospect should buy from you rather than from one of your competitors.

2. What are three things you could do each day to ensure that you eventually become one of the best salespeople in your industry?

3. What are your three most important goals in life, business and personal, right now?

4. What are the three essential tasks you must carry out each day to ensure high levels of sales for your company?

5. List three activities in the 1000-Percent Formula that you are going to start doing every day.

6. In what three ways could you position yourself as a consultant in every customer conversation?

7. What one skill would help you the most to increase your sales and your income?

CHAPTER SIX

Financing Your Business

The successful person makes a habit of doing what the failing person doesn't like to do.

—Thomas Edison

OUR ABILITY TO DO ACCURATE COSTING FOR YOUR PRODUCTS
and services, and then to set proper prices for what
you sell, can make all the difference between profits and losses,
success and failure.

The name of the game is "profit." Everything you do in your
business, every number that you calculate and consider, every
point of focus and concentration must be aimed at generating
profits of some kind.

Profits can be defined as "the excess of revenues over
costs." You earn a profit when you sell a product or service at a
price that is greater than the total cost of bringing that product or

service to market. Always remember the Japanese proverb, "Making money is like digging in the sand with a pin; losing money is like pouring water on the sand."

Become a Numbers Person

Most entrepreneurs are motivated by ideas, concepts, hopes, desires, and optimism. They like to interact with people, to market and sell. They enjoy negotiating, communicating, and persuading. They are action-oriented and like to be in continuous motion. They start early, work hard, and stay later. Often entrepreneurs will work for months and years, seven days a week, 10, 12, and 14 hours per day to turn their dreams of entrepreneurial success into reality.

But most entrepreneurs are not "numbers" people. They have little patience for the details of financial statements and accounting. They are eager to get on with the business of meeting with people and selling the product. In fact, for most entrepreneurs, dealing with numbers is irritating and frustrating.

But nonetheless, for you to move solidly along the way to wealth, to become a successful entrepreneur, and eventually, a self-made millionaire, you must master the numbers in your business. You can hire bookkeepers, accountants, and financial advisors to help you, but you can never abdicate the responsibility of fully understanding every penny and every dollar that comes in and out of your business.

Get the Facts

Harold Geneen of ITT once said, *"Get the facts. Get the real facts. Not the hoped for facts, the assumed facts, or the possible facts. Get the real facts. Facts don't lie."*

It is absolutely essential for your success that you know the financial facts of every aspect of your business, especially your costs to produce and offer your product or service and the prices you charge for what you sell. It is amazing how many businesses, large and small, are operating on the basis of false assumptions and incorrect numbers. Sometimes they joke and say, "We lose money on everything we sell, but we make it up on the volume." But this is not a joke.

Determining Your Costs

Often the person who makes the fewest mistakes in business is the one who succeeds the most. You don't have to be an entrepreneurial genius to be successful. You just have to master your numbers and know what you are doing.

> Often the person who makes the fewest mistakes in business is the one who succeeds the most.

You have heard the old saying, "You can't get there from here." When you do an accurate cost analysis for a new product or service, you will often find that, based on what you can charge for that product or service in the current market, you can't make a profit on it. It makes no sense to go through all the time and trouble of bringing this product to market because the return is too low. The potential for loss is too high. The possible profits are not as great as you could earn by offering something else.

One of the keys to entrepreneurial success is to offer a high-margin product or service of some kind. It is to produce, acquire, sell, or distribute a product or service from which you earn high profits on the sale of each one. In this way, you have a substantial cushion built in to protect you from losses.

Be Brutally Honest with Yourself

In determining your costs, you must be brutally honest with yourself. You must include every single cost that will be incurred in the process of satisfying your customer. You must include the costs of the product; the costs of marketing, advertising, and selling the product; the costs of delivering and servicing the product;

and the after-sales costs of repairs, maintenance, and returns for any reason. Once you have totaled up all of these costs, you should then add a "fudge factor" of 10 percent or 20 percent to give yourself a buffer against unexpected costs that will pop up in spite of your best efforts to avoid them.

There are several costs that you must consider:

1. Direct costs. These are the costs of goods sold. If you make a product or buy it from a manufacturer or distributor for $5, including all costs of shipping, transportation, insurance, and delivery, and you sell the product for $10, your cost of goods sold is $5. This is fairly easy to calculate.

2. Indirect costs. These are the costs that are attributable to all of the products or services that you sell, not any specific ones. Indirect costs can be costs of salaries, rent, telephones, utilities, marketing, advertising, shipping, delivery, and many others.

Specialist companies make a good living by going into businesses and analyzing the true direct and indirect costs of producing and selling each product or service. Many business owners are astonished to find that a product that they thought was profitable is actually costing them money each time they sell an item because of "unattributed costs."

Include Every Expense

Upon inspection, it may turn out that the cost of executive time, staff salaries, advertising, sales costs and commissions, shipping and delivery, insurance, and returns because of product defects or dissatisfied customers actually total up to a loss on every sale. This is why it is so important that you continually calculate and recalculate every dollar that you must spend per product or service that you sell.

You need to consider the costs of returns, both shipping and delivery. You need to calculate "shrinkage," the cost of your products or services that "disappear" in the course of business activities. You need to calculate breakage and defects. You need to calculate losses that come from writing off accounts from people who cannot or will not pay you for what you have sold them. In totaling your indirect costs, you need to determine how much you must allocate for follow-up services, maintenance, and repairs for the product or service you sell.

In addition, you must calculate the outside services that you require to operate your business, especially legal and accounting. In addition, you must calculate not only the labor costs and salaries of each staff member who must spend any amount of time producing, selling, or delivering any product or service, but you must also include *your own labor* at your hourly rate.

The average entrepreneur works about 2,000 hours per year. If your income target is $50,000 per year, divide it by 2,000 to get your desired hourly rate of $25. If your income goal is $100,000 per year, your hourly rate is $50.

The average entrepreneur works about 2,000 hours per year. If your income target is $50,000 per year, divide it by 2,000 to get your desired hourly rate of $25. If your income goal is $100,000 per year, your hourly rate is $50. In determining your indirect costs, you must include the number of hours of your individual time that go into achieving the ultimate sale. Otherwise, your true costs will be distorted and inaccurate.

3. Fixed costs. These are the costs that you incur each month whether or not you sell a single item or generate a single dollar of revenue. Your fixed costs include salaries for your permanent staff, rent, utilities, many operational costs, and the costs for outside services, plus your own personal income from the business.

You should calculate your fixed costs regularly to determine how much it costs you to stay in business if you have no revenues at all. One of your business goals should be to continually find ways to reduce your fixed costs.

4. Variable costs. These are the costs that increase or decrease depending on your level of business activity. These costs are incurred only when a sale takes place. They can include costs of goods sold, sales commissions, delivery costs, and other costs that can be attributed, directly or indirectly, to the cost of each product or service you sell.

5. Semi-variable costs. These are costs that are partially fixed and partially variable. They can include part-time labor when you are busier than normal, additional utility, telephone, and mailing costs, and additional costs for outside services.

6. Sunk costs. These are expenses that you have incurred that are *gone forever*. They can never be recovered. They are like an unattached anchor thrown overboard that sinks to the bottom of the ocean and is irretrievable.

Here's an important point. Many entrepreneurs make the mistake of attempting to retrieve their sunk costs. For example, they place an advertisement that generates no response. They then decide to place even more advertisements of the same kind, in the same medium, in order to "capitalize" on the amount they have already lost with an ineffective advertising campaign. They "throw good money after bad." We often refer to this as "pouring money down a rat hole."

Ambrose Bierce once wrote, "Fanaticism consists of redoubling your efforts when you have forgotten your aim."

Building a business is often a sloppy affair. No matter how smart you are, you will buy products that you cannot resell, that no one wants at any price. You will buy furniture that will turn out to be of no value to you. You will run advertisements and engage in other costs that, in retrospect, were a complete waste of money. In building a business, these mistakes are inevitable.

But it is essential that you recognize them for what they are— sunk costs. The money is gone forever. You cannot recoup it. You must not spend a single dollar attempting to compensate for a financial mistake in the past. Focus on the future and on sales and profits. Let the sunk costs go.

Once you have accurately calculated all of these expenses, direct and indirect, fixed and variable, plus semi-variable, you will have a precise cost for bringing each product or service to the market satisfactorily. With this number, you can then begin thinking about your pricing structure.

Pricing Your Products

Sometimes I ask a group of business owners, "Who sets your prices? Who determines your profit margins? Who determines what you offer, to whom you offer it, and how much you sell? Who determines the entire course of your business in a competitive market?"

Almost invariably, the first response I get is "I do!"

Then, I gently point out that this is not true. I tell them, "In reality, your competition determines how much you charge, how much you sell, who you sell it to, your profit margins, how fast you grow, and almost everything else about your business."

Business Is Like Warfare

Business is like warfare in a certain way. In warfare, most strategy is determined by the enemy. It is determined by what you need to do to defeat your enemy and what your enemy is likely to do to counter your actions in order to defeat you.

As an entrepreneur, you must be looking in two directions simultaneously. You must be intensely focused on your customers, on who they are, where they are, what they want and need, what they

> Remember: your competitors get up every single morning and think all day long about how to *put you out of business.*

will pay for, how they buy, and every other factor about them. At the same time, you must be intensely focused on your competitors. Remember: your competitors get up every single morning and think all day long about how to *put you out of business.* They

think about how to undercut your prices and steal your customers. Just as you are focused on sales and profits, so are they.
From the day you begin thinking about being an entrepreneur,
your competitors will have a major influence on every decision
you make and how successful those decisions turn out to be.

Your Goal in Business

Your goal in business is to achieve a "meaningful and sustain-
able competitive advantage." This means that you build into
your product or service specific benefits and advantages to the
customer that no one else offers. You create or discover your
"unique selling proposition." You then seek out those specific
customers in the marketplace who want, need, and are willing to
pay the very most for what it is that you do or offer better than
anyone else. This is the key to business success.

Nonetheless, you need to think carefully about your prices.
Prices are subjective. There are no hard and fast rules for setting
prices on a product or service. There are only "guesstimates" of
what customers will pay and of what the market will bear. Your job
is to determine a price that is the very highest price possible that
you can charge without losing your customers to your competitors.

The Market-Clearing Price

In economics, there is a concept called the "market-clearing
price." This is the price at which all buyers can purchase all the
products or services of a particular kind that they want and at
which all sellers can sell all the products or services that they
offer. At the end of the day, everyone is satisfied: all buyers
have purchased everything they want and all sellers have sold
everything they have offered. This is the ideal price, the market-
clearing price, in any market.

Whenever you see a discount sale at any business, and
especially in retail operations, you see an example where the
people who priced the products guessed wrong. They set a price

that was too high to enable them to sell all they had to offer to buyers at that price. As a result, they are forced to guess again. They must lower the price and attempt once more to clear their stock and recoup their investment.

Sometimes you see a store that will offer more than one series of discounts. They will have a sale, and then another sale at even lower prices. In each case, the storeowners are guessing again and again. They are struggling to find the price at which they can clear their stock, the price at which sellers will buy all they have to offer.

Never Be Overstocked

One of the reasons that Wal-Mart is the most successful retail operation in the world is because of their policy of "Always low prices." Because of their highly sophisticated, satellite-controlled inventory and distribution systems, they are never overstocked in any store.

Every purchase at a Wal-Mart store is immediately communicated by satellite to massive company computers in Bentonville, Arkansas. This information concerning product, size, color, and characteristic is immediately conveyed, again by satellite, to the manufacturers and shippers of the products nationally or internationally. Each factory has up-to-date feedback on exactly which products to produce and exactly which stores to ship them to and in exactly what quantity, color, kind, type, or shape. Wal-Mart is successful largely because it has the most sophisticated distribution system of any retail operation in the world.

When you shop at Wal-Mart, you know that it is unlikely that Wal-Mart will be discounting that product in a clearance sale a couple of weeks from now. You also know that, because of Wal-Mart's ability to purchase in massive quantities, you are probably getting the best price possible for that particular item. As a result, people shop at Wal-Mart with complete confidence, to the tune of almost $300 billion per year.

Pricing Models

There are various ways that you can set your prices for your products or services. But you must always remember that these are "guesstimates" based on your knowledge of what your competition is charging and what your customers are likely to pay, combined with your intuition, your gut feeling, about what the market will bear.

> The "entrepreneurial instinct" that makes you successful is your ability to perceive a gap between what customers will pay for your product or service and the total cost of bringing that product or service to the market.

The "entrepreneurial instinct" that makes you successful is your ability to perceive a gap between what customers will pay for your product or service and the total cost of bringing that product or service to the market. It is this "profit opportunity" that entrepreneurs can see, and that most other people cannot see, that is the spark that triggers entrepreneurial activity. The better you become at identifying this gap between sales price and cost, the more successful you become as an entrepreneur.

Cost Plus Markup

In this model of pricing, you take your total cost for a product or service and mark it up by a specific amount, usually a percentage.

For example, in restaurants it is standard to mark up a bottle of wine 100 percent. If the bottle costs $25 from the wholesaler, the restaurant puts it on the menu at $50.

Depending upon competitive pressures and sales volume, companies will mark up their products with different percentages. For jewelry, for example, because jewelry stores have to carry such large inventories, the markups can be several hundred percent. For groceries, because products turn over so fast, the markups are about 20 percent of wholesale costs. This is a convenient way to set your prices, especially at the beginning. But always keep your competitors' prices in mind.

Cost Plus

When I built my first shopping center, the owner of the construction company explained to me their pricing practice. They said, "We take the total cost of construction and then add 10 percent for administration and 10 percent for profit."

This is cost-plus pricing. Many companies that offer services will total the entire cost, direct and indirect, of providing the service and then mark it up by a fixed percentage. Many contracts, large and small, are done on a cost-plus basis. This might be appropriate for your business, as well.

Multiple of Total Costs

You calculate your total costs of production, or costs of goods sold, and then multiply that by a specific number. If you manufacture a high-margin product or service, you could mark it up by five or even ten times the manufacturing cost. This is quite common.

For example, in book publishing, the retail price of the book is usually equal to seven times the cost of printing the book. If the book costs $3 to print, the retail price in the bookstore will be $21. This is the rule of thumb used in the publishing industry.

Many entrepreneurs do not realize that, because of all of the indirect and unexpected costs in their businesses, they can go broke marking up a product by 100 percent. They can buy a product for $10 and sell it for $20. But once they have deducted all of the various costs that go into getting that product to the customer, they find that they are losing money on every sale. Don't let this happen to you.

Market Pricing

This is perhaps the most common way of setting a price on a commonly used consumer product. Unless your product or service offers a valuable benefit not offered by your competitors, you will have to keep your prices within 10 percent of what your competitors are charging for the same product or service in the same market area.

When I was working in the banking and trust industry, they offered a certain percentage return on fixed deposits. Customers are hypersensitive to even quarter-point increases or decreases in these amounts. All a bank or trust company had to do to increase its deposits immediately was to raise the interest rate that it was paying by one quarter of a point. In a short time, millions of dollars of new deposits would flow to that institution.

In self-storage, for example, the amounts that can be charged for a specific size of storage unit in a particular area are quite uniform throughout that area. People who store their possessions will move from one place to another for a difference in rent of as little as $5 a month. Again, competition sets the prices that you can charge.

Monopoly Prices

These are prices that you can charge because no one else offers the same product or service as you in that market area. As a result, you can charge premium prices, prices that are highly profitable to you, and customers who want your product or service have no choice but to pay you what you demand.

The ability to charge monopoly or above-market prices comes about only because your product or service is unique and irreplaceable. For example, you can often charge monopoly prices simply because of your geographical location, which no one else has.

Convenience stores charge substantially more for their products than large grocery stores. They can do this because they have a monopoly on their location. They are the only store close to the customer and therefore are a quick and convenient place at which to shop. They commonly mark up what they sell by 30 percent to 50 percent and customers willingly pay it.

One of the ways that you can charge monopoly prices is by designing or structuring your products or services in such a way that they are far more attractive and desirable than those of your competitors. You, in fact, become the "only" choice for a potential customer. The customer cannot think of going anywhere else except to your place of business.

In professional speaking, there are thousands of speakers who give talks and seminars on every conceivable subject. The average speaker or trainer may earn a few hundred dollars per day for all the work of travel, preparation, and delivery.

But in this industry, there are "marquee" speakers such as Colin Powell, Norman Schwarzkopf, Bill Clinton, and sports stars who commonly demand and get fees of $50,000, $100,000, and even $150,000 for a keynote talk of less than one hour.

Why is this? It is because there is only one of each of them. Each is a monopoly. If a person wants that speaker, there are no alternatives. If a company or organization wants to book Bill Clinton or George H. W. Bush to speak, it has no choice but to pay the monopoly price.

One of the questions that you must continually ask is "How can I structure my business or my offerings in such a way that I am the preeminent choice for customers in my market?"

What can you do to make your products or services so attractive so that your prospective customers see you as the very best choice of all, the only choice, all things considered? By asking and answering this question continually, you may come up with a special way of doing business that gives you a competitive advantage. This then enables you to charge premium prices and earn premium profits.

Variable Prices

Many companies charge different prices, at different times, for different reasons, for the same product or service. Their prices vary depending upon circumstances.

For example, if you sell a single product or service to a single customer, your costs can be quite high in servicing that customer. In this case, you would charge "full retail."

On the other hand, if your customer were to buy a large volume of your products or services, your cost of servicing that customer would decline dramatically. In this case, you could offer substantial discounts for volume purchases, as many companies do.

You could offer variable prices if people purchased from you more frequently. Frequent flier programs are built around offering bonuses, upgrades, and special services to encourage travelers to use a particular airline more often.

Many companies charge variable prices based on the time of day, week, or even season or year that people buy. For example, if you buy ski equipment in the fall prior to the ski season, prices will be at their peaks. If, on the other hand, you buy ski equipment in the spring and summer, after the ski season, you can buy at substantially reduced prices.

If you go to a vacation resort during the holiday season, the prices will be at their maximum levels. If you visit the same vacation resort during the off-season, the prices are substantially lower.

Many restaurants offer special bonuses, discounts, and two-for-one offers for people who dine on Monday, Tuesday, or Wednesday. Some restaurants offer half-priced bottles of wine on slow nights to attract more customers and to help offset their fixed costs.

Often, companies will have spare capacity. They will have fixed costs of equipment, staff, rent, utilities, and other costs that must be paid. To defray these costs, they will often offer their products or services at deeply discounted prices, just above their total costs, in order to keep the staff working and the factories operating.

In car dealerships, the salespeople are assigned monthly quotas. At the beginning of the month, the quota period has just begun. They will therefore bargain very hard. The salespeople will make every effort to charge you the highest possible price if you go out to buy a car in the first three weeks of the month. Toward the end of the month, the pressure to make quota increases and the salespeople will make whatever concessions are necessary to make a sale. If you are going to buy a car, always go during the last few days of the month. You get the best prices and conditions possible.

Another type of variable price sale is the "add-on" or "upsell." In this case, you can offer your product or service at a special price, as long as the customer at the same time buys something else, on which you also make a profit. For example, Xerox used to sell its copiers at low prices just as long as the customers bought all their high-priced paper from the company, which made most of its profit from the paper, not the copiers.

Consider the hospitality industry as another example. If you want to reserve a hotel room, always phone the hotel *directly*. Do not use the 800 number. People who answer the 800 number, the national reservation service, have no flexibility to negotiate rates.

When you phone the hotel directly, ask for the "very best rate" for a room on the dates that you desire. The first price that the employee will give you will be the "full rack rate," the highest possible rate for that room.

You then ask, "Do you have a lower rate?"

If the hotel is not full for the dates when you want a room, the employees are instructed not to let you off the line. They are taught and trained to get you to reserve a room, at any price. They know that an empty hotel room is of no value to them at all.

When you ask for a lower rate, they will suggest a corporate rate or a rate for a room without much of a view. You then ask again if they have a lower rate than *that*. They will then move down to an even lower rate. With many hotels that are not fully booked, you can continue this process down through as many as seven discounts. This is another form of variable pricing, where they will make every effort not to lose the potential customer.

The Walkaway Price

This is the price *below which* you will not sell your product or service. You should be clear about this number before you begin negotiating. This becomes the basis for your variable pricing. Below this amount, you incur losses that make it of no value for you to offer the product or service at all.

Introductory or Loss Leader Prices

With this type of pricing, you consider the *lifetime value* of a customer. If you know from experience that a customer who buys from you will buy from you several times over the coming months or years, you can often charge a "loss leader price" to acquire the customer. This discount is simply a cost of doing business, a cost of "buying" a customer.

In many cases, it is quite common, especially for retail or service businesses, to lose money on the first sale. Because of the high costs of marketing, advertising, and selling commissions or expenses, plus the cost of goods sold, a business can actually end up with a net loss on a sale once all your costs have been deducted. There's often no choice but to do this.

> It is quite common for professional services firms to offer their services at a 50 percent discount for the first year, if the client will sign a five-year contract.

However, when you calculate the lifetime value of the customer and you are confident that this customer, if satisfied, will buy from you over and over again, you can justify taking a loss on the first sale.

It is quite common for professional services firms to offer their services at a 50 percent discount for the first year, if the client will sign a five-year contract. They will lose money the first time they do business with the client, but they will make it up later. In the meantime, they will keep their people, facilities, and resources busy during the initial period.

Market Demand Pricing

This is charging whatever you feel that the market will pay. If you have a competitive advantage of some kind, you can charge a premium because customers will willingly pay more to get the special features or benefits that you offer. After the Hurricane Katrina disaster, for example, prices for hotels, food, transportation, and many other products of limited supply increased all over the surrounding area because of the sudden surge in demand.

When should you raise your prices? The best time is when the market demand for your products or services is almost greater than your capacity to deliver them.

If you are a service company and you are fully booked, all day long, you can probably raise your prices without decreasing the demand. If people are buying your products with both hands and you cannot keep enough of them in stock, this is a good sign that your products are *underpriced* based on what customers are willing to pay. In this case, you can gradually raise your prices, selectively or across the board. You continue raising your prices for your products or services until the demand slows down and balances out with the quantity of products and services that you are prepared to supply.

Break-even Price

This is the price at which you earn neither a profit nor a loss. You sell the product for exactly what it cost you to produce it. You only sell at the break-even price when you cannot charge any more, and you do not have to charge any less.

Clearance Sale Price

This is the price at which you admit that the market demand for the product or service you have produced is considerably less than you had anticipated. You have too many of your products in stock. They are taking up too much room and selling too slowly.

At the clearance sale price, you bite the bullet and realize that "Half a loaf is better than none." You clear out your stock so that you can turn that "dead stock" into cash that you can then use to offer other products and services that are in greater demand and on which you can earn a greater profit.

Pricing Flexibility

This is an *attitude* more than anything else. Always remember that prices are subjective. They are guesses at what the market will bear. They are based on a variety of pieces of information that are continually changing.

You want to sell as many of your products and services as possible, at the highest possible price, to yield the highest possible profits. But from the beginning to the end of your entrepreneurial career, you must always be flexible with your prices and be prepared and willing to raise or lower them depending on market conditions.

Sometimes, you can increase your prices by a large or small amount and dramatically change the profitability of your business. In other cases, you can lower the price of your products or services and so increase your sales volume at a lower profit point such that your overall profits increase substantially.

For example, if you are selling 1,000 units per month at $10 and making a profit of $3 each, you would be earning $3,000 per month in profit. But if you lowered your price to $9, you might sell 2,000 units per month and earn $4,000 (2,000 x $2 profit per item). In each case, it is a judgment call that you must continually test and measure.

The key is to be *flexible*. Nothing is written in stone. Be open to new information. Be continually watching your competition. Listen closely to your customers. Keep your hand on the pulse of the sales and profitability of your business.

Break-even Pricing

This is one of the most important numbers that you must calculate for every product and service that you offer. Fortunately, it is not particularly difficult, if you have done the proper costing and pricing exercises described above.

In break-even pricing, you first determine the total cost of bringing your product or service to market. If you have a variety of products or services, you calculate the total costs of each one, using the formulas described earlier.

Once you know how much your product or service costs, you then determine exactly how much you can sell it for in a competitive market. You take into consideration all of the volume purchase discounts, losses, breakage, shrinkage, defects, returns, and all other deductions from your sales prices and work out the exact *average* price that you receive for the sale of each item.

To determine your break-even point, you then deduct your total average costs per item from the total average selling price per item. This gives you your *profit contribution.*

Calculate Your Profit Margin

Your profit contribution is also your *profit margin,* often expressed as a percentage. This gives you the exact amount of *gross profit* or *return on sales* that you earn from each sale.

You then total your fixed costs of operation. Remember: these are the amounts that you have to pay each month, whether you make a sale or not. You divide your average profit contribution per item into your monthly fixed costs to determine your break-even point.

For example, if your average gross profit per item sold is $10 and your fixed costs of operation are $10,000 per month, you divide $10 into $10,000 to get a break-even point of 1,000 units.

This means that you have to sell 1,000 units of your product each month to break even. Below that point, you are losing money each month. Above that point, you are earning a gross profit of $10 per item sold.

Reduce Your Fixed Costs

Your goal throughout your business career is to reduce your fixed costs and increase your variable costs. You reduce the costs that you have to pay each month, whether you make a sale or not, and increase your variable costs, the amounts that you have to pay *only* when you make sales.

By doing this, you lower your break-even point as far as you can. The lower your break-even point, the fewer number of units you have to sell each month before you make a profit.

Evaluate Every Expenditure

Once you have determined your break-even point, you evaluate every expenditure against this number. If you are going to advertise, you determine how many of your units you will have to sell in order to break even on a particular form of advertising at a particular cost. If you are going to buy any type of equipment to improve the operations of your business, you calculate how many more of your products you will have to sell in order to break even on that investment. You apply your break-even number to every amount that you anticipate spending, for any reason, to grow your business. This is one of the best "reality checks" you will ever use as an entrepreneur.

> If you are going to buy any type of equipment to improve the operations of your business, you calculate how many more of your products you will have to sell in order to break even on that investment.

Financial Ratios

To be a successful entrepreneur, you must have a firm grasp of the numbers in your business. Over the years, several financial ratios have been developed as tools to help business owners understand the numbers in their businesses with greater clarity.

1. **Gross margin.** This is the amount of profit that you earn after deducting the cost of goods sold and all other direct costs involved in producing and delivering your product or service to your customer.

2. **Net margin.** This is the amount of net profit that you earn per sale or per month after deducting all of the direct, indirect, and attributable costs involved in operating your business.

For example, grocery stores mark up the products they sell by an average of 20 percent. But the average net profit that grocery stores earn on sales is closer to 3 percent. The difference is eaten up by all of the costs involved in running a grocery store.

The average large company in America earns less than 10 percent net profit, usually closer to 5 percent, after all costs of operation have been deducted. This is often called *EBITDA* (earnings before interest, taxes, depreciation, and amortization) or sometimes *EBTIDA* (earnings before taxes, interest, depreciation, and amortization).

Remember: small increases in prices and small reductions in costs can lead to huge differences in profitability. Every dollar that you save in cost reduction goes straight to the bottom line as net profit. Every dollar that you earn in increased prices, holding costs constant, goes straight to the bottom line, as well.

3. **Return on investment (ROI).** This is the total profit, expressed as a percentage, that you earn based on the total amount invested in your business. This total amount includes the money that you have paid out of your own pocket, plus all of the other money that has been invested or borrowed in any way.

4. **Return on equity (ROE).** This is the percentage return that you earn on the money that you have personally invested in the

business. This is usually a more accurate way of determining the profitability of your enterprise.

For example, if you have invested $100,000 of your own money in the business and you are earning a net profit of $10,000 per year, your return on equity is 10 percent. Whenever you calculate potential returns on investment or returns on equity, you must always compare the return from this business activity with the return from any other business activity in which you can invest the same amount of time, money. and energy.

5. Return on sales (ROS). This is another way of calculating your gross margin. It is the percentage of gross profit that you make from each sale. If you buy an item for $1 and you sell it for $2, your *return on sales* would be 50 percent.

6. Return on energy (ROE). This is perhaps the most important calculation of all. This is the return you receive on the amount of physical, mental, and emotional energy you invest in your business. Sometimes this is referred to as your *return on life*. You must be continually aware of how much of your life you are investing in your business. Financial investments can be recouped or replaced, but the amount of your life that you spend on any business activity is gone forever.

Analyze and Compare

The reason that you continually calculate your gross margins, net margins, and return on sales is to compare the various products and services that you offer. The 80/20 rule says that 20 percent of your products and services will yield 80 percent of your profits. You must be absolutely clear which products and services are the most profitable for you to offer. These financial ratios help you develop that clarity.

Watch Your Numbers

In this chapter, we have discussed the most important numbers for you to know and understand in building a successful business on your way to wealth.

Before you make any business decision or investment, you should take the time to achieve complete *accuracy* with regard to the amount you can charge, the prices that people will pay for your products or services, and the exact cost of bringing those products or services to market.

You must be clear about your *break-even point* and continually update and evaluate this break-even point as market conditions, prices, and costs change.

You should continually evaluate your business in terms of your returns on sales, your return on equity, your return on investment, your gross and net margins, and the actual amount that you take home at the end of the day, your return on energy.

You must always include your personal labor as a key cost of doing business. Without your investment of mental, emotional, and physical energy, there would be no business.

Many business owners earn less operating their own businesses than they would if they worked for someone else. Because they do not include the cost of their labor as a real cost of doing business, they understate their costs and expenses and often underprice their products and services. Don't let this happen to you.

Get a Good Accountant

Get a good accountant to calculate these numbers for you. Review them regularly. Be continually looking for ways to reduce costs and increase prices. Be continually seeking ways to increase gross and net margins on everything you sell.

The good news is that the more time and attention that you devote to studying and understanding your financial statements and ratios, the better you will get in this area. The better you get, the better decisions you will make. The better decisions you make, the more profitable your business will become and the faster you will move along the way to wealth.

Action Exercises

1. Calculate for your best-selling product or service exactly how much you receive per sale and how much it costs to service your customer.

2. Examine each of your better-selling products or services and determine if you should raise or lower your prices.

3. Calculate your fixed costs for your business, including your own time, so you know what it costs you to keep your doors open.

4. Calculate the breakeven point for your business and seek ways to lower it each month.

5. Decide what constitutes a "sunk cost" and resolve today not to spend another dollar or minute trying to recoup it.

6. Calculate your own personal hourly rate and compare every activity you engage in against that amount.

7. Decide today to take action in at least one area to increase your prices, make your products more attractive, or reduce your fixed costs.

CHAPTER SEVEN

Becoming a Master Negotiator

Always bear in mind that your own resolution to succeed is
more important than any other one thing.

—Abraham Lincoln

OUR ABILITY TO INTERACT, COMMUNICATE, PERSUADE, AND
negotiate with others determines your income more
than any other factor. You owe it to yourself to become excellent
at getting the best deals whether you are buying or selling. As a
business owner, your ability to negotiate well on your own behalf
can save or make you a fortune over the course of your career.

In a larger sense, all of life is a negotiation. You are always
negotiating in some way. When you drive from one place to
another, you negotiate through traffic, as you let other people get
in front of you and they let you get in front of them. When you
go to a restaurant, you negotiate to get a table, first of all, and
then to get the kind of table you most like. You negotiate all the
elements of your work life and all the things you do or don't do.

157

You negotiate prices, terms, schedules, standards, and a thousand other details all day long. The process is never-ending.

It is not really a question of whether or not you negotiate. The only question is "How good a negotiator are you?"

One of your chief responsibilities in life is to learn how to negotiate well in every situation. You need to be able to get more of the things you want faster and more easily than you could if the other person were better at negotiating than you.

There are several universal principles of negotiating that you can learn and practice that will help you to get more of the things you really want, better, faster and easier than ever before. When you apply these principles consistently, you will improve every aspect of your life.

Something Is Worth Whatever Someone Is Willing to Pay

Many people are confused on this issue. They think that individuals or organizations determine what others will pay. However, even schoolchildren know that something is worth only what someone else is willing to pay for it, no matter what anyone says or demands. Prices are merely estimates set arbitrarily as a guess at what people will pay.

Every discount, markdown of prices, or business bankruptcy is an admission of a failure to guess correctly. The producers of the product or service guessed wrong when they set the price. Customers did not feel that it was worth that price and either bought something else or kept their money.

This is why every negotiation is different and there are no hard-and-fast rules determining buying or selling prices for products or services. All prices are therefore negotiable.

Only the person who is being asked to pay for the good or service or to pay a certain wage is in a position to determine what that thing is worth to him or her. When people say that something *should* be worth a particular amount or someone *should* receive a certain salary, they don't realize that the word "should" is meaningless in negotiating.

All Prices Are Guesses

All prices are established arbitrarily, at least initially. It is only what customers are willing to pay in the marketplace that determines whether those prices are correct. If the prices are too high, the products

> The customer in the marketplace will ultimately decide how much will be paid for everything.

will not sell or the prices will be reduced. The customer in the marketplace will ultimately decide how much will be paid for everything.

Where are you experiencing price resistance in the sales of your products or services? How could you increase the value of what you sell in such a way that a critical customer would choose to pay you more for it? How could you increase your value and attractiveness in such a way that your company or your customers would willingly pay you more for what you do?

Everything Is Negotiable

All prices and terms are set by someone. They can therefore be changed by someone. This does not mean that they will be changed, but it does mean that there is always a chance. When you begin looking at life as one long, extended negotiating process, you will find that almost every situation contains elements that you can negotiate to improve the terms and conditions for yourself and others.

Rule: Prices are a best guess estimate of what the customer will pay. This means that asking prices are only loosely connected to market realities. The cost of manufacturing and marketing a particular product or service often has very little to do with the price that is put on it. Price is arbitrary and merely reflects someone's opinion of what the market will bear at that moment.

Rule: Every price was set by someone and can therefore be changed by someone. Don't be intimidated by written prices, on signs or in letters or contracts. Assume that they are written in pencil and can easily be erased and replaced with something more favorable to you. The key is to *ask*.

Begin today to ask for better prices and terms, no matter what you are offered initially. Make it a game. Ask politely. Ask in a warm and friendly way. Ask positively. Ask expectantly. Ask confidently. But be sure to ask. You will be amazed at how quick people are to improve the prices and terms for you if you ask.

Everyone Wants to Improve His or Her Situation

Human beings are goal-oriented, purposeful in their behavior, whether their aims are clear or unclear. They are always driven or motivated toward achieving "more" of something, although that something may change from minute to minute. This is the entire reason behind buying, selling, and negotiating.

> From infancy to old age, you are *ambitious*. You want to improve your life in some way or some part of your life.

From infancy to old age, you are *ambitious*. You want to improve your life in some way or some part of your life. If you are earning a certain amount of money, you want to earn more. If you have a certain level of physical health, you want to be healthier. If you have a home or an apartment, you want a larger one. If you get a larger one, you want a second one somewhere else. If you have a car, you want a bigger car. If you have a bigger car, you want two cars and perhaps even a motorcycle or a motor home.

It is normal and natural and completely human for each of us to continually strive to get more, better, faster, newer, and cheaper of everything and anything we can think of. The only limitations on human ambition are the limitations imposed either internally, by the limitations that we place on our own minds, or externally, by the limitations imposed upon us by our personal resources, law, and society.

Rule: When you see no way to get more of what you want, you will do nothing at all. For example, you may be driving an old car and are passed on the road by someone driving a $100,000 Rolls-Royce Corniche. You may fantasize and think about how nice it would be to drive such a lovely car, but you can't even begin to imagine earning the kind of money that would enable you to pay $100,000 for a car. Therefore, the sight of the Rolls-Royce may cause you to feel dissatisfied with your current vehicle, but it would not motivate you to take an action of any kind.

The real differences in levels of ambition are explained by differences in ability and opportunity on the one hand and the intensity of desire and belief on the other. If you really believe that you can get from wherever you are to wherever you want to go, you will be continually taking action to move yourself from your current position toward your goals. This is why people negotiate.

Rule: If you are either completely contented or if you feel completely helpless, you will not act to improve your condition. There are two main reasons why people do not continually act to improve themselves and their lives in some way. The first is because they have reached a state of *contentment* where they feel that no further improvement is either necessary or desirable. The second is because they have reached a state of *hopelessness* where they do not think anything they do will make much of a difference.

Identify your own personal ambitions. In what areas are you *dissatisfied* with your situation? Be clear about the better condition that you desire. What steps could you take today to begin moving toward the results that you really want? Where and how could you improve your conditions by negotiating a better situation for yourself?

People Follow the Line of Least Resistance

You place a high value on your time, your money, your mental and physical energy, and your resources. As a result, you do everything possible to conserve them. You use your energies sparingly and you spend them as carefully as possible to get the things you want. You are economical in your choices. You *economize*. You don't spend more than you have to satisfy a particular need or to achieve a particular satisfaction. This is major drive behind every negotiation.

Rule: You cannot consciously choose a harder way to accomplish something over an easier way to accomplish it. You are structured mentally in such a way that you cannot force yourself to select a more difficult path to your goal if you can see an *easier* path, all other things being equal.

Rule: All human beings are inherently lazy in that they follow the path of least resistance to get whatever they want. Laziness is normal, natural, and inherent in all human action. This lazy tendency has led to every great advance and breakthrough in science and technology. It is the driving force behind many negotiations.

How can you position your offerings in such a way that your customers perceive your products or services to be the *easiest* way for them to get the benefits you offer?

What new products or services could you develop that would offer your customers a faster and easier way to get the things they want?

How could you reorganize your life so that you are achieving your goals with less effort? How could you be "lazier" in the very best sense of the word?

People Always Strive to Get the Very Most for the Very Least

This is just a simple and obvious explanation of human behavior under almost all circumstances. However, it is an extraordinarily important law of negotiating for you to know. It enables you to avoid confusion in interpreting and understanding the behaviors of other people. This principle explains why people often start off by asking a ridiculous amount in selling or offering a ridiculous amount when buying.

Rule: When given a choice between more and less, all things being equal, you will always choose more in order to maximize your situation. This is a natural human behavior. You are designed in such a way that you cannot consciously choose *less* pleasure, satisfaction, or fulfillment if you can have *more* for the identical expenditure of resources.

Rule: The desire for more is automatic and instinctive and applies to all human needs, wants, and desires. In other words, you always choose more rather than less. You always maximize your situation. If you are selling something and one person offers you $5 and another person offers you $6, if you are behaving normally, you will choose the offer of $6 rather than the $5. If you accept less rather than more, some other value or consideration must be at work influencing your behavior.

All things being equal, the amount you will demand from the exchange of your time, money, or resources will always be the very most that you can get for the very least that you can give.

This desire for more is another way of saying that everyone is inherently *greedy*. This is just a fact, a universal quality of human nature. In reality, the quality of *greed* has no inherent value, positive or negative. Everyone is greedy in that everyone prefers more to less, all things being equal. People are just greedy for different things.

Everyone Wants More

Parents are greedy for their children in that they want the very best for them in life. Athletes are greedy in that they want to achieve the very most possible in their areas of competition. Everyone is greedy. Everyone wants more. Everyone is looking for ways to improve their conditions in some way. The only thing that stops people from acting on their greed is that they don't see a way to get from where they are to where they want to go.

All buying and selling decisions and all negotiations are based on this principle of maximization. All salaries and wages are determined by it, including yours. Think continually about how you can add value to your products and services, every day, so that you offer maximum value to your customers.

> Think continually about how you can add value to your products and services, every day, so that you offer maximum value to your customers.

Your customers are continually seeking more in every purchase decision. They go where they feel that they are getting the best deal, all things considered. How could you increase the value that your customer perceives in dealing with you?

The Principle of Expediency: People act to get the very most of the things they want in the fastest and easiest way possible without regard to the secondary consequences of their actions. This is the umbrella principle that explains much of how the world really works and why things happen the way they do. This law explains virtually all human behavior, all marketing and sales, all negotiating, and all relationships. It largely explains happiness and unhappiness, success and failure in all areas of human endeavor.

Rule: People are naturally and normally lazy and greedy in everything they do. This is the way people behave in a state of nature. It is neither good nor bad. It is simply a fact. It is value-free. It is only the ways in which a person manifests these natural instincts that make the instincts either positive or negative. These qualities exist in every negotiation, on both sides.

The happiest people are those who accept this law as a basic operating principle for individual behavior. They are not surprised when people act consistently with this law. They expect it. They are amazed and pleased when people act otherwise, perhaps motivated by a higher value or principle, but they don't become upset when it doesn't happen.

The Principle of Expediency explains the way the world works. It is often called the "law of least resistance." Everyone in the world is driven in every conceivable way to seek the fastest and easiest way to get the things they want, right now, without concern for the long-term consequences of their actions.

Examine your behavior honestly and objectively. In what ways do you act expediently to get the things you want? Is this tendency helping you or hurting you?

Examine the behavior of the people you negotiate with. In what ways does the Principle of Expediency explain their behavior?

Study your business. Look at your products and services, your sales and marketing. In what ways are your promotional activities in harmony with the natural tendencies of your customers to act expediently? How could you change your ways of doing business so that they conform more to the way your customers actually make buying decisions? How could you make your business offerings faster, easier, and cheaper for your customers?

The Principle of Futurity: The purpose of business negotiation is to enter into an agreement such that each party's needs are satisfied and each is motivated to fulfill his or her part of the agreement and to negotiate with the other party in the future. This is a foundation principle of negotiating and applies especially to negotiations where you will be dealing with the same party again. In business, it is quite common for people to be in and out of business transactions and negotiations with each other for many years. This fundamental futurity must be kept in mind at each stage of each negotiation.

Let's break this law down into its constituent parts.

First, "the aim of a negotiation is to enter into an agreement." It is assumed, but not always true, that both parties want to do business together. If one does not and is merely negotiating for some other purpose, the other party can be at a considerable disadvantage.

The second part says, "such that each party's needs are satisfied." This means that an agreement that causes one or the other party to feel that he or she has *lost* does not fulfill the basic requirement of a successful negotiation. Both must feel that they have come out ahead.

This principle then goes on to say, "... and each is motivated to fulfill his or her part of the agreement and to negotiate with the other party in the future."

This means that both parties are satisfied enough with the outcome that they are motivated to fulfill whatever commitments they have made and they feel positively enough about the agreement that they are willing to negotiate again and enter into subsequent agreements in the future.

Analyze your current negotiating style. In what areas have you been more focused on "winning" in the short term without really considering the long-term damage that you might be doing to the relationship? What could you do to change this immediately?

Look for ways to make the final agreement more acceptable to the other party. Think of negotiating with this party again in the future based on the terms and conditions you are finalizing today. How could you improve the terms without sacrificing things that are important to you?

The Principle of Win/Win or No Deal: In a successful negotiation, both parties are fully satisfied with the result and feel

that they have each "won" or no deal should be made at all. You should always seek an outcome that satisfies both parties to the negotiation if you are going to be doing business with this party again in the future. Remember: you always reap what you sow. Any settlement or agreement that leaves one party dissatisfied will come back to hurt you later, sometimes in ways that you cannot predict.

In every ongoing negotiation or business relationship, you should aim for a win/win solution or no deal. When you enter into a negotiation with this person again, you should make it clear in advance that you are committed to reach a solution that is satisfactory to both. If it does not entail a win for both parties, you should simply refuse to make any deal at all.

> In every ongoing negotiation or business relationship, you should aim for a win/win solution or no deal.

When you are determined to achieve a win/win solution to a negotiation and you are open, receptive, and flexible in your discussions, you will often discover a third possibility that is superior to either of the two proposed solutions.

This kind of third alternative solution is almost always achievable if you are willing to look for it. It simply requires a commitment to win/win.

Both Parties Should Be Happy

Once you've decided that you are going to agree only to a settlement that is satisfactory to both parties, this mean that you do not have to accept any arrangement that you consider second best. With your values and your intentions clear, you are now in a position to utilize every strategy and tactic available to you to get the very best deal for both of you, one that ensures that you both end up happy with the arrangement.

Think win/win in all your interactions with others, at work and at home. Actively seek a middle way that satisfies the most pressing desires of both parties. Be creative in suggesting alternatives that get both you and the other person more of what you each want.

Examine any situation you are in today that you are not happy with. How could you restructure the terms and conditions in such a way that the other person gets more of what he or she wants as you get more of what you want?

The Principle of Unlimited Possibilities: You can always get a better deal if you know how. You never need to settle for less or feel dissatisfied with the result of any negotiation. There is almost always a way that you can get better terms or prices, whether you are buying or selling. Your job is to find that way.

Rule: If you want a better deal, ask for it. The word "ask" is the most powerful word in the world of business and negotiating. Most people are often so paralyzed by the fear of rejection and disapproval that they are afraid to ask for anything out of the ordinary. They just accept what is offered to them and hope for the best.

But this is not the case with the best negotiators. The top negotiators will quite calmly and confidently ask for any price or terms remotely within reason. You will be quite astonished at the better deals you will get by simply asking for a lower price if you're buying and asking for a higher price if you're selling.

Rule: Whatever the offered price, react with surprise and disappointment. Remember: most people have plucked the price out of the air. They are always asking for more than they expect to get or offering less than they expect to pay. In either case, you should *flinch* and react with mild shock, no matter what the price or the offer. Appear hurt, as if the person has just said something cruel or unkind that was totally uncalled for. Then ask, *"Is that the best you can do?"* And remain perfectly silent.

Very often, when you ask a person how much an item costs and you flinch when he or she gives you the price, that person will lower the price immediately. In almost every price is a cushion of potential discount; very often the salesperson will drop to that price with one painful flinch on your part.

Rule: Always imply that you can do better somewhere else. There is nothing that causes a seller's price to drop faster than for you to say that you can get the same item cheaper from another source. This shocks the seller and shakes his or her self-confidence. The seller immediately feels that the deal is slipping away and often cuts the price quickly.

> The more examples you can offer when you demand a lower price, the faster the other party will come down to a price that is acceptable to you.

Do your homework. Check around and ask about other prices that are available. The more examples you can offer when you demand a lower price, the faster the other party will come down to a price that is acceptable to you.

The Law of Four: There are four main issues to be decided upon in any negotiation; everything else is dependent on these. There may be dozens of details to be ironed out in a complex agreement, but the negotiation will succeed or fail on no more than four issues. I have spent two and three days in negotiating sessions with teams of skilled businesspeople on both sides of the table, discussing 50 pages of small and large details, only to have everything boil down to four key issues at the end.

Rule: 80 percent or more of the value of the negotiation will revolve around these four issues. This Law of Four and this factor of 80 percent turn out to be valid in almost every case. No matter how long or complex the negotiation, no matter how many clauses, subclauses, details, terms, and conditions, in the end, most of the discussion and the most important points of the negotiation revolved around four basic items.

Rule: Of the four main issues in any negotiation, one will be the main issue and three will be secondary issues. For example, you may decide to buy a new car. The four main issues to be decided might be price, trade-in value of your current car, color, and accessories. Warranty and service policies will be important but secondary.

The Law of Four works only when the other party's order of importance of the four issues differs from yours. One party may be more concerned about price and the other party may be more concerned about terms. This can lead to an excellent win/win solution that satisfies the most important needs of each party.

Think of something expensive and complex that you have purchased in the past. What were your four key considerations? What were the considerations of the other party? How did you finally reach an agreement?

Think of an upcoming negotiating situation in your work. Make a list of all your considerations and then order them by importance to you. Make a list of the other party's considerations in order of importance. How can you use this information to get a better deal?

The Principle of Time Preference: People prefer to satisfy a want, need, or desire sooner rather than later. Time is your most precious resource. It is like money: your supply is limited. Because you value your time and your life, you always want to achieve your goals with the smallest expenditure of time. You always negotiate to get what you want as fast as you can.

Rule: When choosing between a reward today and that reward at some future time, unless there is an excellent reason, you will prefer it earlier rather than later. If someone says to you, "I can give you $1,000 today or I can give you $1,000 tomorrow," which would you choose?

The answer is obvious. If you have the choice, you will prefer it *now* rather than *later*. Why? There are two main reasons. First, you don't know what might happen between today and tomorrow. And second, it is worth more to you today because you can do something with the money immediately. Both the predictability and the possible pleasure are greater if you get the money today.

Rule: Everyone is impatient to have more, faster, and easier, because time has a value and sooner is more valuable than later. This natural impatience, based on time preference, is a key consideration in every negotiation. The more impatient the other person is for the negotiation to conclude, the better the deal you can get for yourself.

Time is the currency of the day. People want things faster and faster and they will patronize anyone who offers to satisfy their needs sooner.

How could you speed up the delivery of your products or services to your customers? How could you serve your customers faster? How could you streamline your processes to give your customers more of what they what they want faster than your competitors? Speed is a value that customers will pay for in a negotiation. How could you use speed as a bargaining tool?

The Principle of Timing: Timing is everything in a negotiation. A negotiation can be made or unmade by the time at which it takes place. There is a "too soon" and a "too late" in every situation. Whenever possible, you should plan strategically and use the timing of the negotiation to your advantage. There is a better time to buy and a better time to sell in almost every case. And when your timing is right, you will always get a better deal than when it is not.

Rule: The more urgent the need, the less effective the negotiator. If you are in a hurry to close a deal, your ability to negotiate well for yourself diminishes dramatically. If the other person is eager to make the deal, he or she is functioning under a disadvantage that you can exploit to your advantage.

For example, every company has sales targets for each month, each quarter, and each year. Sales managers are tasked with hitting these numbers. Their jobs, their incomes, and their bonuses depend on it. Every salesperson has a sales quota for each month as well. Therefore, when you are buying any large-ticket item, you will almost always get the best deal if you wait until the end of the month, when the pressure is on to hit the targets.

Rule: A person who yields to time pressure will get the worst of the bargain. Rushing or using time pressure is a common tactic in negotiating and you must be alert to other people trying to use it on you. People will often tell you that you have to make up your mind quickly or it will be too late. If so, you should take a deep breath and patiently ask questions to find out just how urgent the situation really is.

If someone insists on an immediate decision, you can reply by saying, "If you must have an answer now, then the answer is 'no.' But if I can take some time to think about it, the answer may be different."

On the other hand, you can use this tactic to your advantage by running out the clock so the other person has no time left and has to make a decision on your terms. Just don't let someone else do it to you.

Rule: You resolve 80 percent of the vital issues of any negotiation in the last 20 percent of the time allocated for the negotiation. Probably because of Parkinson's Law, which says, "Work expands to fill the time allotted for it," most of the key issues in a negotiation get jammed into the final phase of the discussions. Up to this part of the negotiation, there seems to be a natural human tendency to procrastinate on resolving the most important issues.

> You must be *patient* in a negotiation. You must be prepared for the key issues to be resolved at the last minute.

This means that you must be *patient* in a negotiation. You must be prepared for the key issues to be resolved at the last minute. Setting a schedule and a deadline for a decision will help. If it happens that the key issues are resolved earlier, you can be pleasantly surprised. But this is the exception, not the rule.

When you negotiate, set deadlines for the other party whenever possible. Remember the rule in sales: "No urgency, no sale!" You can always extend the deadline if the other party balks or disagrees.

Try to keep the other party from setting deadlines for you. Whenever possible, state that you are not going to make a decision today, no matter what is agreed to. Give yourself at least 24 hours to think it over before deciding. Sleep on it as a matter of course. You will be amazed at how much better you think when you have put some time between yourself and a major decision.

The Principle of Terms: The terms of payment can be more important than the price in a negotiation. Many products, such as homes and cars, are sold more on the terms of payment and the interest rates than on the price or even the product itself. People usually buy the most expensive home they can qualify for. People buy the most expensive car they can afford. Your ability to vary the terms can be the key to success in a negotiation.

Rule: You can agree to almost any price if you can decide the terms. If you really want to purchase an item or sell an item and the negotiation is stuck on the price, shift the focus of your discussion to the terms and try to either lengthen or shorten the payment term.

Rule: Never accept the first offer, no matter how good it sounds. Even if the first offer is everything you could possibly ask for, don't accept it. Act a little disappointed. Ask for time to think it over. Ponder the offer carefully. No matter how good the first offer is, it usually means that you can get an even better deal if you are patient.

Rule: Never reject an offer out of hand, no matter how unacceptable it sounds at first. You can turn a bad offer into a good deal if you can dictate the terms of payment. You can say, "That is an interesting suggestion. It is not quite what I had in mind. But let's see if there is a way that we can make it work."

Remember that you can get a better deal by controlling either the price or the terms. If the other party is determined to get the very best price possible, you can agree by suggesting terms that make the price acceptable.

Always look for ways to extend the actual payment of money as far into the future as possible. Any delay or deferment of payment, especially if you can arrange for no penalty for pre-payment, makes the deal more attractive by lowering the cash outlay in the present.

The Principle of Preparation: Eighty percent or more of your success in any negotiation will be determined by how well you prepare in advance. Action without planning is the cause of every failure. Negotiating without anticipating what the other party might want is the cause of just about every poor deal. The very best negotiators are those who take the time to prepare the most thoroughly and to think through the situation completely before the negotiation begins.

> The very best negotiators are those who take the time to prepare the most thoroughly and to think through the situation completely before the negotiation begins.

Rule: Facts are everything. The devil is in the details. It is the details that trip you up every single time. Be sure to get the facts *before* you begin negotiating, especially if the subject is large or complicated—or both. Don't be satisfied with the apparent facts or the supposed facts or the obvious facts or the hoped-for facts or the assumed facts. Insist on the real facts and all of them, because the facts don't lie.

Avoid the temptation to accept superficial answers or incomplete numbers. Don't leap to conclusions. Avoid wishful thinking.

Do your research, ask questions, listen carefully, and take notes. This can make an extraordinary difference in the outcome.

Rule: Do your homework; one small detail can be all you need to succeed in a negotiation.

Rule: Check your assumptions; incorrect assumptions lie at the root of most mistakes. For example, one of the assumptions that almost everyone makes when going into a negotiation is that the other party *wants* to make a deal. This may not be the case at all. You need to test this assumption.

Sometimes the other party has already decided to deal with someone else or not to buy or sell at all. Perhaps the other party is just going through the motions of negotiating to see how good a deal he or she can get. Maybe someone else has offered to match the very best offer you can make. The other party may be negotiating without the authority or the ability to follow through on any deal you agree to. Be sure to check your assumptions before you invest too much time or emotion.

Always *think on paper*. Write down every single detail of the upcoming negotiation. Note every term and condition you can think of. Then, identify your assumptions and begin gathering information to verify or reject them.

Whenever possible, talk with someone else who has negotiated the same sort of deal with the same person. Find out what the other person is likely to want and what he or she has agreed to in the past. Be prepared!

The Principle of Authority: You can negotiate successfully only with a person who has the authority to approve the terms and conditions you agree upon. One of the most common of all negotiating ploys is called "agent without authority." This is a person who can negotiate with you but who is not authorized to make the final deal. No matter what you two agree upon, the agent without authority must check back with someone else in order to confirm the terms of the agreement.

Rule: You must determine in advance if the other party has the authority to make the deal. The simplest way to do this is to ask the person if he or she is authorized to act for the company or client. If not, you must be cautious about the positions you take and the concessions you offer.

Rule: When dealing with someone who cannot make the final decision, you must represent yourself as being unable to make the final decision either. Fight fire with fire. If the other person says that he or she cannot make the final decision, you claim to be in the same position: anything you agree to will have to be ratified by someone else. This tactic levels the playing field and increases your flexibility in the case of an unacceptable counteroffer.

Make every effort to find out who makes the final decision before you begin negotiating. Ask the person you are talking with if he or she is empowered to enter into an agreement based on what you discuss. If not, find out who has the power and attempt to speak with him or her directly.

When you cannot deal with the final decision-maker, do everything possible to find out exactly what he or she will find acceptable in making this decision. Be sure to mention that you will also have to get final approval before you can make an irrevocable decision to proceed. Keep your options open whenever possible.

The Principle of Reversal: Putting yourself in the situation of the other person enables you to prepare and negotiate more effectively. Before any negotiation that involves a good deal of money or a large number of details, use the lawyer's method of reverse preparation. This is a great technique that dramatically sharpens your negotiating skills.

In law school, future lawyers are often given a case to either prosecute or defend as an exercise. They are then taught to prepare the opposing attorney's case before they begin preparing their own. They sit down and examine all the information and evidence and they imagine that they are representing the other side. They prepare that side thoroughly with the full intention of winning. Only when they feel that they have identified all the issues that the opposing attorney will bring up do they then begin to prepare their side of the case.

You should do the same. Before you negotiate, write down everything that you think may be of concern to the other party. Writing things down clarifies them and enables you to see possibilities that you might otherwise have overlooked. When you have identified the major concessions that you think the other party will want, you can then think about what you will offer in exchange. You can see where you are strong and where you are weak. You can identify areas where agreement or compromise may be possible. This type of preparation by reversal is the hallmark of the superior negotiator.

Think through, discuss, and write out every concern or demand that you feel the other party might have *before* you meet and begin negotiating. Test these assumptions by asking the other party about his or her concerns and requirements.

The Principle of Power: The person with the greater power, real or imagined, will get the better deal in any negotiation. Your ability to recognize both your power and the power of the other party is critical to your success in negotiating. Often you have more power than you know. Often the other party has less power than he or she appears to have. You must be clear about both.

Rule: No one will negotiate with you unless they feel you have the power to help them or hurt them in some way. You must have something the other person wants or you must be able to withhold something he or she wants in order for the other person to take you seriously. You must be continually thinking about the situation from the other's point of view so that you can position yourself for the maximum benefit to yourself.

Rule: Power is a matter of perception; it is in the eye of the beholder. You can often create the perception of power, of being able to help or hinder a person in some way, by being bold and creative. Often when I am getting poor service on a flight or at a hotel, I will take out my pen and a piece of paper and politely but coldly ask the other person, "May I have your name, please?"

This reaction invariably draws people up short. They hesitatingly offer their name while they mentally scramble to figure out who I might be and why I might be asking. I then ask them for the correct spelling. I carefully write the information down and put it away. From that moment on, the service improves dramatically. Whoever it is cannot take a chance that I might be a senior person in the company or someone who personally knows a senior person.

There are various types of power that you can develop and use, either individually or together, to influence and persuade the other party in any negotiation. The more important the issue to be negotiated, the more time you should take to consider how you can use one or more of these elements of power to strengthen yourself and your position.

1. *The power of* **indifference***:* The party who appears to be the most indifferent to whether or not the negotiation succeeds often has power if the other party wants more for the negotiation to succeed. As a rule, you should always appear slightly detached and indifferent in a negotiation, as though you don't really care one way or the other.

2. *The power of* **authority***:* When you have an impressive title or you look as though you have the authority to make decisions, this image alone often intimidates the other person and enables you to get a better deal. A powerful *image* can really help convey authority. Dress excellently, in every respect. Dress with power, in strong, conservative colors, looking like the president of a major corporation. When you look like a million dollars, the other party, especially if he

or she is not as well dressed, will often be intimidated into giving you a better deal or will be much more responsive to your demands.

3. *The power of* **expertise:** The power of expertise comes from your making it clear that you are extremely *well informed* on the subject under negotiation. A person who is perceived as an expert in any situation has power over those who do not feel as knowledgeable. And the more research and preparation you have done in advance, the more knowledgeable you sound.

4. *The power of* **empathy:** Human beings are predominantly *emotional* in everything that they do and say. In negotiations, a person who feels that the other person empathizes with him or her and his or her situation is much more likely to be flexible and accommodating in the negotiation. The popular image of the tough-talking negotiator is largely fictitious. Every study of top negotiators shows that they are highly empathetic, low-keyed, solution-oriented, and pleasant individuals to do business with. Good negotiators are usually very *nice* people. They make it clear from the beginning that they really care about finding a solution that all parties can live with.

5. *The power of* **rewarding or punishing:** When other parties perceive that you have the capacity to help them or hurt them, they are usually far more cooperative than if they don't feel you have this power.

With each of these five powers, your choice in negotiating is either to be influenced *by* or to have influence *over* the other party. The more you can develop and use these powers to your advantage in a negotiation, the more persuasive and effective you will be.

Prior to your next major purchase, sale, or negotiation of any kind, review the forms of power described here and think about how you can use them to gain an advantage. Write out and discuss your thinking with someone else to be sure that you are completely prepared.

Practice the power of indifference in every negotiation as a matter of course. When you appear unconcerned or uninterested in the success of the negotiation, you will often unnerve the other party and induce concessions from him or her before you have even taken a position or made an offer.

The Principle of Desire: The person who most wants the negotiation to succeed has the least bargaining power. The more either you or the other party wants to make the purchase or sale, the less power that person has. Skilled negotiators develop the art of appearing polite but uninterested, as if they have many other options, all of which are as attractive as the option being negotiated.

Rule: No matter how badly you want it, you should appear neutral and detached. The more important it is to you, the more important it is for you to appear *unemotional*, unaffected, and unreadable. Don't smile or appear interested in any way. An attitude of mild boredom is best.

Rule: The more you can make the other party want it, the better the deal you can get. This of course, is the essence of successful selling. Focus all your efforts on building value and pointing out the benefits the other party will enjoy from the purchase or sale. Desire is the critical element.

> Focus all your efforts on building value and pointing out the benefits the other party will enjoy from the purchase or sale.

Before you begin negotiating, list all the benefits of dealing with you. Organize the list by priority, from the most persuasive benefit to the least persuasive. Mention these key benefits in the course of the negotiation and be alert to the reaction of the other party.

Always be polite and friendly during the negotiation. This makes it easier for you to change your mind, to make concessions, and to compromise without your ego getting in the way. It also makes it easier for the other party to make concessions and agree at the appropriate time.

The Principle of Reciprocity: People have a deep subconscious need to reciprocate for anything that is done to or for them. This Principle of Reciprocity is one of the most powerful of all determinants of human behavior. When someone does something nice for us, we want to pay him or her back, to reciprocate. We want to be *even*. Because of this, we seek an opportunity to do something nice in return. This principle is the basis of the law of contract, as well as the glue that holds most human relationships together.

This Principle of Reciprocity is most active in negotiating about concessions. Ideally, every concession in a negotiation should be matched by a concession of some kind by the other party. The giving and getting of concessions is often the very essence of a negotiation.

Rule: The first party to make a concession is the party who wants the deal more. You must therefore avoid being the first one to make a concession, even a small concession. Instead, be friendly and interested, but remain silent. The first person to make a concession will usually be the person who makes additional concessions, even without reciprocal concessions. Most purchasers or sellers are aware of this. They recognize that early concessions are a sign of eagerness and are prepared to take advantage of it. Be careful.

Rule: Every concession you make in a negotiation should be matched by an equal or greater concession by the other party. If the other party asks for a concession, you may give it—but never without asking for something else *in return*. If you don't request a reciprocal concession, the concession that you give will be considered to have no value and will not help you as the negotiation proceeds.

If a person asks for a better price, suggest that it might be possible but you will have to either decrease the quantity or lengthen the delivery dates. Even if the concession is of no cost or value to you, you must make it appear valuable and important to the other party or it will not help you in the negotiation.

Rule: Small concessions on small issues enable you to ask for large concessions on large issues. One of the very best negotiating strategies is to be willing to give in order to get. When you make every effort to appear reasonable by conceding on issues that are unimportant to you, you put yourself in excellent field position to request an equal or greater concession later.

Use the Principle of Reciprocity to your advantage. Before negotiating, make a list of the things the other party might want and decide upon what concessions you are willing to give to get what you want. This preparation strengthens your negotiating ability considerably.

The Walk-Away Principle: You never know the final price and terms until you get up and walk away. You may negotiate back and forth, haggling over the various details of the deal for a long time, but you never really know the best deal you can get until you make it clear that you are prepared to walk out of the negotiation completely.

Rule: The power is on the side of the person who can walk away without flinching. If you get up and walk out, be pleasant, low-keyed, and polite. Thank the other person for his or her time and consideration. Leave the door open so that you can enter back into the negotiation with no loss of face.

Rule: Walking out of a negotiation is just another way of negotiating. Some of the very best negotiators, both nationally and internationally, are extremely adept at getting up and walking out. They will leave the room, the building, the city, and even the country if necessary, to strengthen their positions and increase their perceived power in a negotiation.

A common tactic, when teams are negotiating, is for one or more of the key players on one team to get up angrily, storm out of the room, and vow never to come back. However, at least one player will stay behind and then seek some way to make peace with his or her partners and bring them back into the discussion. The remaining party will be friendly and accommodating, as if he or she is really on the side of the other party. This tactic is very common in labor-management negotiations and in international relations.

Before you enter into a negotiation, be prepared to get up and walk out. If you are negotiating as a team, make sure all players know about this tactic and when to use it. At the appropriate moment, you all stand up and head for the door. This will often completely confuse and disorient the other party or parties.

Be prepared to cut off a negotiation the very minute you get an unacceptable offer or condition. Close up your briefcase, thank the other person for his or her time, and head for the door. The better you get at walking away, the better the deals you will get.

> The better you get at walking away, the better the deals you will get.

The Principle of Finality: No negotiation is ever final. It often happens that once a negotiation is complete, one of the parties thinks of something or becomes aware of an issue that has not been satisfactorily resolved. Maybe circumstances change between the signing of the agreement and its implementation. In any case, one of the parties is not happy with the result of the negotiation. One party feels that he or she has "lost." This is not acceptable if the two parties are anticipating negotiating and entering into further deals in the future.

Rule: If you are not happy with the agreement, ask to reopen the negotiation. Most people are *reasonable*. Most people want you to be happy with the terms of the negotiated agreement, especially if the terms are to be carried out over a long time. If you find that you are not happy with a particular term or condition, don't be reluctant to go back to the other person and ask for something different.

Think of reasons why it would be beneficial to the other person to make these changes. Don't be afraid to point out that you are not happy with this situation and you would like to change the agreement so that it is more fair and equitable to you.

Rule: Use zero-based thinking on a regular basis by asking yourself, "If I could negotiate this arrangement over again, would I agree to the same terms?" Be willing to examine your past decisions objectively. Be prepared to ask yourself, "If I had not made this agreement, knowing what I now know, would I enter into it?" This ability to engage in zero-based thinking, to get your ego out of the way and to look honestly and realistically at your ongoing situation, is the mark of the superior negotiator.

Review your current situation and especially those ongoing arrangements with which you are dissatisfied in any way. Think about how you could reopen the negotiation and what sort of terms and conditions would be more satisfactory to you.

Whenever you experience stress or unhappiness with an agreement, or whenever you feel that the *other party* is dissatisfied, take the initiative to revisit the agreement and find a way to make it more satisfying for both parties. Think long term.

Summary

Negotiating is a normal and natural part of life. You owe it to yourself to become very skilled at it. As with any skill, the key to excellence is to practice at every opportunity. Make it a game.

Ask for what you really want. Ask for better prices, better terms, better conditions, better delivery—better everything. Realize that you can save yourself the equivalent of months and even years of hard work, by learning how to become an excellent negotiator. And you can if you think you can. You can if you just *ask*.

Action Exercises

1. Make a list of the three areas in your business or personal life where you negotiate the most often. How could you improve your results in each of these areas?

2. What are three types of power that you could develop in an upcoming negotiation?

3. What are the three main advantages of preparing thoroughly in advance of a negotiation?

4. What are three motivations that each person has in any negotiation?

5. List three tactics that you could use in a negotiation to improve your bargaining position and the results you achieve.

6. Review the deals you are in today and determine which of them you should go back and renegotiate.

7. Practice negotiating daily by continually asking for better tables in restaurants, better prices when you are selling or buying, and better terms in every purchase or contract. Never be afraid to ask.

CHAPTER EIGHT

Improving Your Personal Productivity

He who every morning plans the transactions of the day and follows out that plan, carries a thread that will guide him through the labyrinth of the most busy life.

—Victor Hugo

 OUR ABILITY TO MANAGE YOUR TIME WELL IS ONE OF THE CRIT-ical skills for personal and business success. All successful people are described as being "very well organized." Successful people are more productive than unsuccessful people. Successful people get more and better results in less time and with less energy and effort than unsuccessful people.

The good news is that time management is a skill that can be learned, with repetition and practice. When you learn and practice the key skills of time management, they soon become a habit.

When you develop the time management habits of successful people, you will double and triple your productivity and you will double and triple your results and rewards as well.

Key Points on Managing Your Time

1. Time management is really life management. As Peter Drucker said, "You cannot manage time; you can only manage *yourself.*" And how well you manage yourself will determine your results, your rewards, and even your peace of mind.

2. The quality of your time management determines the quality of your life. I used to think that time management was a skill that I could practice occasionally, whenever I thought about it. I saw time like a planet orbiting around the sun of my life. Then I learned that time management is the sun of my existence and everything I do revolves around it. Everything requires time.

3. Time is necessary for accomplishment. All work requires time. All success requires time. Time is necessary for relationships. Time is the one indispensable resource. It cannot be stored up or saved.

The rule is that you cannot save time. You can only *spend it* differently. You can only reallocate your time from activities of low value to activities of higher value.

4. Time management is a skill that can be learned and must be learned. It is a skill like driving a car or typing on a keyboard. It takes a good deal of time, effort, and discipline to develop good time management habits, but once you have developed them, they will then serve you for the rest of your life.

Practice One Skill at a Time

When you make a commitment to manage your time more effectively, you should select just one area, one time management skill, one habit, and work on that single-mindedly for a full month.

Do not try to improve several things at once. Just select the one habit that can help you the most at this time. Practice every single day, without exception, for 21-30 days. By that time it will have become a permanent part of your behavior. Then you can move on to the next time management habit.

If you develop one new time management skill per month, in a year you will have developed 12 skills or more. The quality of your life will have been transformed. You will be two or three times more productive, earning more money and taking more time off.

The Situation in Your Life Today

1. You have too much to do and too little time. If you are running your own business or working in a business, you probably have as many as 200 or 300 hours worth of tasks, projects, reading requirements, and other things backlogged. No matter how fast or efficiently you work, there is never enough time in the day to get everything done.

2. Your workload and responsibilities continue to increase. It is as though life were a conveyor belt carrying jobs for you to do. The conveyor belt continues moving, hour after hour, day after day. It never stops. No matter how much you get done, there is always something new coming down the line.

> No matter how much you get done, there is always something new coming down the line.

And the more you get done, the more responsibility will flow to you. It has been said, "If you want something done, give it to a busy man or woman." When you become highly productive and efficient, you will crunch through more work than anyone else around you. As a result, you will attract more work, and usually work that pays more and offers greater opportunity. But the workload will never decrease.

3. You will never get caught up. Many people think by learning and practicing time management techniques, they can find some "magic bullet" that will enable them to get caught up with all their tasks and responsibilities. This is a myth. The fact is that you will never be caught up. There will always be something more to do.

Here's the rule: the only way that you can get control of your time and your life is to *stop doing* certain things. You cannot do more things. You can only discontinue activities of low value or no value.

Successful people do fewer things than unsuccessful people. But they do the most important things and they do them well. They do them quickly and efficiently and on schedule.

The 80/20 Rule

The Italian economist Vilfredo Pareto concluded in 1895 that society could be divided into two groups, the "vital few" and the "trivial many." He found that, in every society, 20 percent of the people, the "vital few," owned and controlled 80 percent of the wealth, while the other 20 percent of the wealth was dispersed among the remaining 80 percent, the "trivial many."

Today we apply the Pareto Principle to every aspect of work. It says that 20 percent of your activities will contribute 80 percent of your value. 20 percent of your customers will represent 80 percent of your sales. 20 percent of your products will contribute 80 percent of your profits. 20 percent of your people will produce 80 percent of the value of all your staff.

> 20 percent of your products will contribute 80 percent of your profits. 20 percent of your people will produce 80 percent of the value of all your staff.

What this means is that, if you make a list of ten tasks that you have to accomplish in a day, two of those tasks will be worth more than the other eight together. Here is the worst part. Each of the ten items may require the same amount of time to accomplish, but in terms of real value and contribution, two of those items will be worth at least five times as much as any of the other items.

Most people divide their work time by the *number* of jobs they have to complete in a day. Top people, however, divide their work time by the *value* of the tasks they have to complete in a day.

Each day, before you begin a task, ask yourself, "Is this task in the top 20 percent of things that I could be doing, or is it in the bottom 80 percent?"

Priorities vs. Posteriorities

A *priority* is defined as something that is more important than something else. It comes first. It has greater value than another task.

A *posteriority,* on the other hand, is something that you do later, if at all. It is done after you have done everything else.

To have enough time to concentrate on your priorities, you must set clear posteriorities in every area of your life. You must decide what you are *not* going to do so that you have enough time to complete those tasks that are vital to your business and your future.

Remember the rule: *"The very worst use of time is to do very well what need not be done at all."*

Make a List

The starting point of excellent time management is to make a list of all the things you have to do. All top time managers work from a list, for every week, every day, and every project. They think on paper.

When you write out everything you have to do on a list before you begin, your work appears more organized and takes on a different perspective. You can see it laid out in front of you. You gain greater clarity as to what is more important and what is less important. You feel a greater sense of personal control.

According to time management specialists, you will increase your productivity by 25 percent from the first day that you begin working from a list, if you are not doing so already. You will gain two extra hours of productive time. Because you are working from a list, you will have a track to run on, all day long.

> **A**ccording to time management specialists, you will increase your productivity by 25 percent from the first day that you begin working from a list.

Like a person traveling across a strange country with an excellent map and a GPS system, you will always know exactly where you are by continually referring to your list.

When something new comes up, before you act on it, write it down on your list. Never do something that you have not written down, not even returning a telephone call.

As you complete each task, tick it off. By the end of the day, you will have a written record of accomplishment in front of you. This list with most of the items ticked off is a source of pride and accomplishment. It makes you feel competent and effective. It makes you feel efficient, with your time under control.

If you don't work from a list, you will be pulled back and forth all day long, with every phone call and interruption. At the end of the day, you will have no record of accomplishment. You will feel stressed out. Working from a list solves all these problems.

Organize Your List

There are two ways to organize your list.

The first is both simple and powerful. Many people have gone from rags to riches with this method. Andrew Carnegie, at one time the richest man in America, said that the following method was more responsible for his success in business than any other technique he learned. Here it is.

Once you have listed all the things that you have to do on a particular day, review the list and ask yourself this question, "If I could do only one task on this list before I was called out of town for a month, which one task would I be sure to complete?"

Put a "1" next to the answer to that question.

Then ask the question a second time, "If I could do only one more task before I was called out of town for a month, which second task would I be sure to complete?"

Put a "2" next to your answer.

Ask this question five more times to determine the top *seven* tasks, in order, that you would want to complete before leaving town for a month. This will give you a clear picture of your most important priorities—and your posteriorities as well.

Then, first thing in the morning, begin on your number-one task. Work at it steadily until it is complete and then go on to your number-two task. If something comes up and you are temporarily distracted, be like a gyroscope returning to center. Return your major task and work steadily away until it is finished.

By your own definition, anything else but your number-one task is a *relative* waste of your time. You have already decided that all other tasks are of lesser value. In terms of high productivity and performance, you can perform at your best only when you are working on your most important task.

The ABCDE Method

Perhaps the most important word in time management is *consequences*. Something is important to the degree to which it has high potential consequences for completion or incompletion. Something is unimportant if there are no consequences involved, whether you do it or not.

> Perhaps the most important word in time management is *consequences*.

Making a large sale or completing a major proposal for a client is something that can have enormous potential consequences for yourself and your business. Getting another cup of coffee or reading the newspaper has no consequences at all.

The tragedy is that most people spend their the time chatting with co-workers, reading the paper, surfing the Internet, drinking coffee, going for lunch, attending "happy hour" at the end of the day, and deciding what they are going to watch on television in the evening. People who think in this way, concentrating on activities that have no potential consequences for their life or work have a limited future.

> People who concentrate on activities that have no potential consequences for their life or work have a limited future.

Discipline yourself to apply the ABCDE Method to your list before you begin working.

A = something that you *must* do. Place an "A" next to each task that has *serious* potential consequences for completion or incompletion. These are the most important jobs on your list. If you have more than one "A" task, set priorities rating them A-1, A-2, A-3, and so on.

B = something that you *should* do. Place a "B" next to the tasks for which the consequences would be mild or there would be no consequences if you do them or do not do them. This type of task may be something like returning a phone call or checking your e-mail.

C = things that are *nice* to do. Place a "C" next to each task that has no consequences at all: whether you do it or not will make no difference. It is something "nice to do" but largely irrelevant to your work and your company. A "C" item may be reading the newspaper, getting another cup of coffee, or chatting with someone in the office. It doesn't matter at all whether you do them or not.

The rule is that you should never do a B task if there is an A task to do and you should never do a C task when there is a B task that is not complete. You must continually discipline yourself to keep focused on those tasks with the greatest potential consequences.

D = things to *delegate*. Put a "D" next to every task that you can give to someone else. The rule is that you must delegate every lower-value task as possible so that you can free up more time for your "A" tasks.

> Many of the tasks that you work on habitually are tasks of low value.

Many of the tasks that you work on habitually are tasks of low value. At one time, they may have been important, but now, they are less important than other things that you need to do and you can delegate them. Which of your tasks deserve a D?

E = things to *eliminate*. Rid yourself of everything that you possibly can to free up time for your most important tasks. The rule is that if it does not have to be done now, it has to *not* be done now.

Be strict with yourself. What tasks could you eliminate altogether with no consequences to the achievement of your most important business and personal goals? These low-value or no-value tasks are candidates for "creative abandonment." These are the *posteriorities* that you set in your life. These are the activities that you must stop doing in order to free up time for the things that you must get done to fulfill your potential and achieve your goals.

The Law of Three

There are five to seven key result areas for every job, seldom more. These are the things that you absolutely, positively must do in order to get the results that are required. What are they for you?

There are many things that you do in your work, day in and day out. If you were to make a list of all your tasks and activities for a week or a month, you might come up with 20 or 30 functions that you perform in your job.

The law of three applied to your work says, however, that of all the things you do there are only *three* key tasks that contribute 90 percent or more of your value to your job and your company. Everything else you do is a support task or a complementary task—

> The law of three applied to your work says that of all the things you do there are only *three* key tasks that contribute 90 percent or more of your value to your job and your company.

you do it as part of your job but it does not contribute most significantly to your value. What are your three main tasks?

In our Focal Point Advanced Coaching and Mentoring Program, we teach a simple way to determine what a person does that contributes the most value to his or her work and life. First we have each person list all the things he or she does in a month at work. We than have each person review his or her list and ask this question: *"If I could do only one thing all day long, what one task on this list would contribute the most value?"*

The answer to this question will usually jump out at you. Once you have determined the one thing, put a circle around that task.

You then ask, *"If I could do only two things on this list, all day long, what would be number two?"*

Put a circle around your answer to that question as well.

You then ask this question one more time: *"If I could do only three things on this list all day long, what would be the third task that contributes the most value to my work and my business?"*

These three tasks constitute your "Big Three." These are the tasks that you absolutely, positively have to do, and do well, to make a maximum contribution to yourself, your job, and your career. These are the three tasks that make the greatest difference and have the most significant *consequences* when you do them or not.

Three Important Questions

There are three important questions that you must ask yourself every day, and throughout the day, to keep focused and on track. Always think in terms of the word *contribution*. The answers to these questions are the things that you can do that make the greatest contribution to your business.

1. Why am I on the payroll? What results are expected of you? What do you do that contributes sufficient value to your business to justify your income?

If your child were to ask you, "Mommy, Daddy, why do they pay you money where you work? What do you do to deserve the money?" what would you say?

Every job, whether you own the company or work for the company, is an agreement to perform a function that contributes value of some kind. In exchange for the value that you contribute, you receive a certain amount of money. What is it that you do that constitutes real, monetary value for your business?

Throughout the day, you should continually ask yourself, "Is what I am doing right now the answer to the question, 'Why am I on the payroll?'"

2. "What can I, and only I, do that, if done well, will make a real difference?" The answer to this question will change as the situation around you changes, but asking and answering it will help to keep you focused on the day. There is always something that *only you* can do, at each moment, that is more important than anything else.

This is a task that no one else can do. If you do not do it, it will not be done by someone else. But if you do it, and you do it well, it can make a real difference to your business or to your personal life. What is it?

3. "What is the most valuable use of my time right now?" This is the fundamental question in all of time management. Every exercise that you go through, every analysis that you conduct of your work, every key result area that you study is to determine the answer to this question: *"What is the most valuable use of my time, right now?"*

Every hour of every day and throughout each hour, you should be asking yourself this question. You then make sure that whatever you are doing at the moment is the answer. It is the most valuable thing you could possibly be doing.

Sometimes after one of my time management programs people will make a game of going around in their companies and asking each other, "Is that the most valuable use of your time right now?" It is a great question that enables you to focus and concentrate on exactly those tasks and activities that can make the greatest contribution to your life.

Use the TRAF System to Handle Paper

Throughout your business life a never-ending stream of mail and paperwork will pour into your office and flow over your desk like a river. Your ability to manage this paper flow is essential to managing your time and concentrating your mental and emotional resources on the most valuable things you can be doing.

There is a simple, four-part formula for managing paper called the TRAF system:

T = Toss: Immediately trash every piece of mail or paper that comes across your desk that is not important or relevant to your work. This includes junk mail, unwanted subscriptions, and copies of data that you don't need for your work. Always have a wastebasket handy so that you can quickly get rid of unimportant, inessential material.

R = Refer: Pass along all mail and incoming information to anyone else who can handle it faster or easier than you. Resist the temptation to deal with it personally just because you know what to do and are comfortable with it. Whenever possible, refer it to someone else who can take care of it for you.

A = Act: Take action on critical letters and pieces of information immediately. These are the essential tasks that can have positive or negative consequences if you don't act right away. If you cannot take action immediately on an important task, get a red file folder and put that piece of paper into this "Action File" for attention as soon as you can get to it.

F = File: Put away those papers and materials that you will need later. Before you do, always ask, "If I need this information at a later time, can I find it anywhere else?"

If the information is easily available elsewhere, toss it. Fully 80 percent of letters and documents that you file will never be needed again. And each time you decide to file something, you are creating work for someone else who has to do it. Only file things that you are sure that you will need again and that you cannot find somewhere else.

Managing Technology

Technological tools such as the Internet, the Blackberry, the PDA, and Microsoft Outlook are meant to organize and streamline your life, not complicate it further. They are meant to be servants, not masters.

Today, the Blackberry is often called the "Crackberry," because people become addicted to using it nonstop. They are continually sending and receiving e-mails and information, all day long.

> Today, the Blackberry is often called the "Crackberry," because people become addicted to using it nonstop.

Almost as if they were addicted, they cannot seem to stop themselves from continually referring to their Blackberries and using them for instant correspondence.

The key to getting control of your PDA or Blackberry is to turn it off regularly. Break the habit of being controlled by the next person who sends you a message. Turn it back on when it is convenient to you and respond to messages in your own time.

The Internet is another tool that can provide instant information from anywhere in the country or around the world. But you must resist the temptation to build your schedule around the Internet. You do not need to get up in the morning and rush to check whether anyone has sent you a message. You do not need to be on the Web constantly as if some life-or-death event is about to take place.

One of my coaching clients, a businessman with divisions in 29 states, found himself on the Internet an average of five hours per day, from the first thing in the morning, throughout the day, until late in the evening. The time he was spending handling his messages was taking him away from far more important tasks and activities that he needed to do and causing him tremendous stress.

We coached him into using the TRAF system in conjunction with his secretary. He was willing to try anything. He sat down with her and went through the 200-300 e-mails that had accumulated in the last 24 hours. He showed her first of all which ones to delete immediately. This quickly eliminated 75 percent of all his e-mails. He then showed her which e-mails should be forwarded to members of his staff to handle. He pointed out to her the e-mails that he had to *personally* take action on and showed her how to handle the most common questions and requirements. Finally, he showed her which e-mails she could put into a separate file for him to review later.

After he spent two hours training his secretary in this TRAF method of dealing with e-mails, she took over his e-mail account. At our next coaching session, he told me that he was now saving 23 hours per week in dealing with e-mail, with no problems or omissions or negative feedback from his customers and clients.

He was able to use that extra 23 hours to more than double his personal income over the course of the following year.

Four Ways to Change Your Life

There are only four ways to change your life and your work. Everything that you could do or refrain from doing can be put under one of these headings.

1. You can do more of certain things. What should you do more of? You should do more of those things that have the highest pay-off, those activities that are working successfully to bring you the results that you want.

> You should do more of those things that have the highest payoff, those activities that are working successfully to bring you the results that you want.

The natural tendency of many people is to work for months and years to find a success formula—and then to promptly abandon it and try something new and different. For example, many people will find a consistent, predictable way to generate leads and convert those leads into customers. They will work hard to build up the reputation and sales volume of a fast-moving, profitable product. And then, for some perverse reason, they will stop doing what is working so well and start trying something else.

What things should you be doing *more*?

2. You could do less of other things. What should you do less of? Obviously, you should do less of things that are *not working*. You should spend less time selling products or services that are hard to market and have low margins. You should do less of things that are not giving you the kind of rewards and satisfaction that you might have expected, even though they might have been successful in the past.

What things should you be doing *less*?

3. You can start doing something completely new. It is hard for most people to break out of their comfort zones and introduce new products or services or try out new ways of doing business. Starting something new requires courage and resilience, especially since most new things don't work, at least at the beginning.

Based on what you've read so far, what things should you *start* doing to improve your business and personal life?

4. You can stop doing certain things altogether. This is sometimes the greatest time-saver of all. Simply discontinue an activity that consumes a lot of time but contributes very little value to your life or your work.

Remember: *your dance card is full.* Before you embark on something new, you must discontinue something old. Before you pick something up, you must put something down. Before you get into a new activity, you must get out of an old activity. Before you begin any new task, you must ask yourself, "What task am I going to have to curtail, downsize, or abandon completely in order to have the time to do this new job?"

Get Better at Your Key Tasks

The law of three says that there are three primary activities that contribute most of the value you give to your company. The quality and quantity of the work you do in these areas are a critical determinant of your success. What are they?

One of the best time-saving techniques of all is to get better at your key tasks. The better you become at an important task, the more of it you can do in less time. The more of it you do, the better you will become and the fewer mistakes you will make. When you become excellent in a key area, you get more and better results and make an even greater contribution.

If, for example, prospecting and lead generation is vital to the sales and profitability of your business, commit yourself to becoming better and better in those areas. Read, listen to audio programs, and attend seminars. Ask for advice from people who are doing well in those areas. Test new methods and techniques. Set goals and targets, measure your success, and self-correct. Resolve to become absolutely excellent in lead generation until you have so many prospects that you do not have enough time in the day to talk with them all.

Profit from the Learning Curve

The highest-paid businesspeople in our society are those who have taken the time to become absolutely excellent at the most important things they do. As a result, they move down what is called the *learning curve* or *efficiency curve*.

> The highest-paid businesspeople in our society are those who have taken the time to become absolutely excellent at the most important things they do.

When you start at the top of these curves, it takes tremendous time and effort to accomplish even a small result. But as you get better and better, you move down the curve, achieving the same results with less and less time, effort, and expense.

At the bottom of the efficiency curve, you can make more sales in one day than you used to make in a week. You can generate more sales and income in a week than you could originally generate in a month. Your business can generate more profits in a month than you used to earn in a year. And this is because you have become extremely good at performing those key functions that contribute most of your sales and profitability. What functions are key for you and your business?

Hire Competent People

You cannot do everything yourself. When you begin, you will have no one to whom you can delegate, but as you grow your business, hiring and keeping excellent people is the key to leveraging and multiplying yourself. It is a great time management tool.

The purpose of a business organization is to maximize strengths and to make weaknesses irrelevant. It is to bring together people of complementary talents and combine their talents to produce a greater result than the same individuals ever could working alone.

Every competent person, including you, has more weaknesses than strengths. There are more areas in which you are average or mediocre than areas in which you are good or excellent. Your job is to identify those few things that you do extremely well and then hire other people to do those things that they do extremely well.

> There are more areas in which you are average or mediocre than areas in which you are good or excellent.

I mentioned in the preceding chapter the principle of constraints. This says that there is almost always a chokepoint or bottleneck—sometimes called the *limiting factor*—that determines the speed at which you achieve a particular goal,

Most likely, the limiting factor in your business growth will be your ability to attract and keep excellent people to perform key functions that are not among your major strengths.

It takes time to find, interview, and select good people, but it can be one of the best time-savers of all. One good person in a key job can help move your company ahead rapidly and free you up to do those critical tasks that only you can perform.

Seven Steps to Improve Productivity

There are seven ways to increase your personal productivity every day. You must practice them over and over until they become automatic:

1. Do things faster. Pick up the pace. Develop a bias for action, a *sense of urgency*. A fast tempo is essential for success. Walk a little faster, move a little faster, and react a little more quickly to problems and opportunities.

The faster you move, the more ground you cover. The faster you move, the more you get done. The faster you move and the more you get done, the better you get at your key tasks. The better you get, the more you get done in the same time. The faster you move and the more you get done, the more positive and motivated you will feel. All successful people are intensely action-oriented.

2. Work longer, harder hours. Start a little earlier, work a little harder, and stay a little later. If you start one hour before everyone else, work through lunch, and stay one hour later, you will expand your workday by about three hours. These three extra hours alone will enable you to double your productivity, performance, and output.

If you come in an hour earlier, you will beat the traffic on the way to work. If you stay an hour later, you will beat the traffic on the way home. If you work through your lunch hour, you will not be interrupted. Altogether, you will have almost three full hours of uninterrupted working time to get on top of your work and ahead of your responsibilities.

It has been estimated that two extra hours of work each day will move you into the top 10 percent of your field within five years. And if you structure your day properly, you will not even notice the extra time you are putting in.

3. Do more important things. Some things that you do are worth five and ten times as much as other things that you do. Many things that you do in the course of the day are not worth anything at all. Fully 50 percent of working time is wasted, even by managers. It is lost in idle conversations with co-workers, personal telephone calls, personal business, coming in late, leaving early, and wasting time at lunch and coffee breaks. But this is not for you.

Focus all of your time and attention on your highest-value activities, those things that only you can do that will make a real difference. Focus on your "A" tasks, those jobs that have the greatest possible consequences. Always work on the most valuable use of your time and you will easily double your output, sometimes in as little as 24 hours.

4. Do things you are better at. You have special talents and skills, based on education and experience, that make you *exceptional* in certain ways. There are things that you can do quickly and easily that are difficult for other people. One of the ways to increase your productivity dramatically is to do those things that come naturally and easily to you. These are tasks that you can complete quickly and well, whereas others may take hours and not do as well.

In my twenties, I became a copywriter for a major advertising agency. I spent many hours studying and writing advertising copy for newspapers and magazines. Because of my experience, today I can write excellent copy, quickly and easily. In my company, whenever we need to write an advertisement, a brochure, or any promotional piece, I can sit down and produce powerful, punchy, effective advertising copy. This is simply something that I am better at. One of my staff might take hours to write something I could write in a few minutes and write better.

5. Do things together. Use the power of *synergy* to get more done. When several people work together on the same job, each person does a small part of the job and so the group produces more than any one member would alone.

Your ability as a business owner to develop a team of people who work together efficiently and effectively to produce and sell your products or services to your customers is the key to your growth and prosperity on the way to wealth.

6. Delegate and assign all lower-level tasks. Think continually about your *hourly rate*. How much do you intend to earn each hour? How much are you worth? Delegate all tasks to anyone who can work at a lower hourly rate than you.

The ability to delegate effectively is one of the most important skills of business management. It requires time, thoughtfulness, and patience. When you learn to delegate the right tasks to the right people in the right way, your own personal productivity will surge.

7. Eliminate all low-value or no-value activities altogether. This technique can save the most time and improve productivity the most.

There is an old saying, *"I cannot do all things, but I can do one thing, the most important thing, and I can do it now."*

Ruthlessly cut back or discontinue any task or activity that is not a high-value use of your time. Remember: time is money. Every hour you spend is the equivalent of spending your hourly rate. Guard your time jealously and refuse to do things that do not contribute to your most important goals.

> Guard your time jealously and refuse to do things that do not contribute to your most important goals.

Perhaps the most powerful word in time management is the word "No!" If a task is not the most valuable use of your time, refuse to do it. Delegate it, outsource it, or eliminate it, whichever is appropriate. But keep focused on the few things that only you can do that will make a real difference. Don't lose time to things that make no difference at all.

Single-Handle Every Task

One of the most powerful time management techniques of all is *single-handling*. This requires that you make a list, organize the list, set priorities, and then work single-mindedly on the most important task that you can possibly be doing at that moment.

You must discipline yourself to overcome procrastination and focus all your time and attention on completing your most important task before you do anything else. This is one of the hardest of all disciplines to learn—and it is the most important single discipline for success in business.

All of business life is a series of projects. Projects are, by definition, *multitask jobs*. They are large and important. As a result, these are the jobs on which you have a natural tendency to delay, defer, and procrastinate. This is a tendency that you must overcome.

Never give in to the temptation to clear up small things first. Select your most important task, assemble everything you need to complete that task, get started, and then work single-mindedly until it is finished.

The Incomplete Action

Psychologists have determined that the "incomplete action"—something that you have started but not yet finished—is a major source of stress and fatigue, often leading to headaches, back pains, and other psychosomatic symptoms..

There exists, deep within each person, a "compulsion to closure," a deep-down desire to finish tasks that we have begun. This "sense of closure" around a major task is absolutely essential for you to feel positive, effective, and on top of your work.

> There exists, deep within each person, a "compulsion to closure," a deep-down desire to finish tasks that we have begun.

Each time you complete a task, your brain releases a small amount of endorphin. This is called nature's "happy drug." In other words, task completion gives you a sense of happiness. It makes you feel more positive and personable. It releases your energy and creativity. A tiny secretion of endorphin in your brain raises your self-esteem and increases your level of personal motivation.

The Big Payoff

Here is the key. When you complete a small task, you get a small secretion of endorphin. If you clear off your desk, assemble and submit all your expenses for the week, or complete a letter to a customer, you feel an immediate sense of pride and satisfaction.

The bigger the task, the bigger this "endorphin rush." When you complete a major, important task, something that only you can do and that can make a real difference to your company, your brain releases a large dose of endorphin. You feel happy and exhilarated. Sometimes you feel like laughing out loud. Your energy levels surge. You feel more excited and enthusiastic about your life and work. Your self-esteem increases. You feel like a *winner*. You feel powerful and effective. You feel on top of your world and capable of doing many other tasks.

The payoff for starting and completing major jobs is therefore tremendous. Not only can it make a tremendous difference in your level of personal success, but it can also give you a tremendous feeling of happiness and personal satisfaction. This is the main reason why you must work to develop the discipline of task completion until it becomes a habit. Once you develop this habit, your productivity will jump and your success will be assured.

The Great Truth

The great truth is that *no one is smarter than you and no one is better than you*. People who are doing better than you in life at the current moment are not smarter or better. They have just figured out the right things to do, in the right way, and they are doing them, over and over, and getting better results than you are—for now.

All business skills are *learnable*. All sales skills are *learnable*. All moneymaking skills are *learnable*. You may not be able to play a violin like Igor Stravinsky or dunk a basketball like Michael Jordan, but you can learn any business skill you need to learn to achieve any business result that you desire to achieve.

It is hard to learn a new skill. It takes time, attention, patience, and discipline. But once you have learned a new skill, you can use it over and over again. And each time you use a new skill, you get better and better at it.

There Are No Limits

As you get better and better in a particular skill area—whether it is marketing, sales, negotiating, customer service, or producing quality products and services, it becomes easier and easier. You get more and better results in less time. What used to take you a month now takes you only a day. What used to take you a year you can now do in a month. Your income and profits go higher and higher. You accomplish more and more, easier and easier. You stomp on your mental accelerator down the road to wealth.

Action Exercises:

1. Develop a complete business plan that shows your cash requirements for the next 12 months; what are they?

2. Develop high, medium, and low sales estimates for your business for the next 12 months; what are they?

3. Determine three different ways that you could get the money you need based on the ideas discussed in this chapter.

4. What three methods could you use to finance your business with other people's money, such as your customers or suppliers?

5. What could you do today, and for the indefinite future, to achieve and maintain an excellent credit rating?

6. What are three of the key factors that banks look for when deciding whether or not to lend you money?

7. What are three of the key numbers you should have every day in the operation of your business?

CHAPTER NINE

The Keys to Entrepreneurial Success

A goal properly set is halfway achieved.

—Zig Ziglar

S I MENTIONED EARLIER IN THIS BOOK, THERE ARE ALMOST nine million millionaires in the United States now (2006) and most of them are self-made. Fully 80 percent of these millionaires achieved their wealth from starting and building successful businesses or by selling for a new business. And what hundreds of thousands and millions of other people have done, you can do as well.

What you have learned in these pages can save you thousands of dollars and many months, or even years, of hard work in making your business a success.

Not long ago in Dallas a young entrepreneur told me that he hadn't known one of these ideas—and that ignorance had cost him eight years of frustration, fruitless effort, and more than $100,000 in lost money.

A young man from Tampa told me he began listening to these ideas on cassette when he was unemployed and living at home. Today he is a millionaire with businesses in three states.

A woman in Sacramento told me that she started using these ideas when she was divorced and broke. Today she has a company with 32 staff, a new husband, a beautiful home, and a big bank account.

You Have to Pay the Price

I have personally paid dearly to learn these key lessons. After working for different companies for 15 years, I thought I was ready to start my own business, so one day I just did it. That was probably the only thing I did right at the beginning, getting started.

Over the next two years, I spent or lost everything I had acquired in my adult life. I learned to sell again. I sold my house. I sold my car. I sold my furniture and everything else that anyone would pay me for. I borrowed from my friends and family to put food on the table for my wife and two little children.

Then I got smart. I began asking, "Why are some businesses more successful than others?" I set out to find the answers.

I read everything I could find and tried it out. I listened to audio programs and attended seminars. I asked for advice from other entrepreneurs and applied that advice to my business. Gradually I turned my business around.

Today, I have a multimillion-dollar business with activities in 17 countries. I live in a beautiful home on a golf course in San Diego. In the last 25 years, I have taught these principles to the executives and staff of more than a thousand companies, from small entrepreneurial businesses to *Fortune* 500 corporations. What I have proven is that these ideas are simple, practical, and easy to apply. Individuals and organizations that apply these strategies increase their sales and cash flow, reduce their costs, and boost their profits, sometimes in a matter of weeks.

Action Is Everything

What you have learned can help you more than you can imagine, when you take these ideas seriously and put them to work.

You've heard it said that 80 percent of new businesses fail in the first two years. Well, 90 percent of businesses started by people who know what they are doing are still going and growing five years later. This should be your goal as well.

This is the age of the entrepreneur. More people are starting more businesses in more fields today than ever in all of American history. And what other successful entrepreneurs and business people are doing, you can do as well, if you just learn how.

> Successful business people are usually just ordinary people who have figured out how to do it right before their competitors did.

Remember this. Successful business people are not smarter than you are and they are not better than you are. They are usually just ordinary people who have figured out how to do it right before their competitors did.

Let's review the most important things you have learned in *The Way to Wealth*.

1. Decide Exactly What You Want

The most important word in success is "clarity." You must be absolutely clear about what you really want from your business. You must be clear about what you are doing and why at every step of your business and personal life. It has been said, *"Fanaticism is redoubling your efforts after your aim has been forgotten.*" And the definition of insanity is *"Doing the same thing over and over again and expecting to get different results."*

Successful businesspeople are intensely goal-oriented. They know exactly what they want and they are working toward achieving their goals every single day. As a result, they accomplish far, far more than the average person in every area of life.

You will be successful starting and building your own business only if you are crystal clear about why you are doing it and how it fits in to the rest of your life. The more you think about your goals and how to achieve them, the more efficient and effective you will be.

Seven Steps to Achieving Goals

Here's a simple, seven-part goal-setting formula you can use to set and achieve any goal in your business life.

1. *Decide exactly what you want.* Most people never do this.

2. *Write it down.* A goal that is not in writing is merely a wish or a fantasy.

3. *Set a deadline* and, if the goal is big enough or will take a long time, set sub-deadlines.

4. *List everything you must do to achieve your goal,* whether it is a certain level of sales, profitability, or any other objective of your business or personal life.

5. *Organize your list into a plan by setting priorities on the activities.* Decide what you should do first, what you should do second, and so on. Decide what is more important and what is less important.

6. *Take action on your plan* immediately. Develop a sense of urgency. Do it now! All successful entrepreneurs are intensely action-oriented. They are busy all the time doing things that move them toward their goals.

7. *Do something every single day that moves you toward your most important goal,* whatever it is at that time. Develop the

power of *momentum* in your personal and business life. Once you get going, keep going until your goal is achieved.

Your Goal-Setting Exercise

Here is perhaps the best goal-setting exercise you will ever learn. You can practice it, over and over again, throughout your career. Take a blank sheet of paper and list ten goals that you want to achieve in the next 12 months.

Write your goals in the present tense, as if they were already a reality, and start every goal with the word "I." For example, you would write, "I sell $xx of my product or service each month" or "I earn $xx profit each month."

Once you have your list of goals, select the one goal that could have the *greatest positive impact* on your business if you were to achieve it.

Take that number-one goal, your *major definite purpose*, and write it at the top of a separate sheet of paper. Then, set a deadline and make a plan. Next, take action on your plan—and resolve to do something every single day until you achieve that goal.

This simple exercise will keep you focused, enable you to concentrate your powers, unleash your creativity, increase your energy, and change your life. Just give it a try and see for yourself.

2. Determine if Entrepreneurship Is Right for You

Only about 10 percent of people are suited to start and build businesses. The other 90 percent are much happier and much more effective working with other people within larger businesses or organizations. You must decide if you are cut out to be an entrepreneur, at the very beginning, if you are going to be successful in the long run.

The primary motivation for becoming an entrepreneur is not money but *freedom*. To succeed as an entrepreneur, your desire for personal freedom and personal control must be so great that it overwhelms all of the other sacrifices and difficulties you will experience. The average entrepreneur works 60 hours a week, six or seven days a week, and often long into the night. When you start a business, you must be prepared to work hard, hard, hard for four to seven years before you achieve the financial success you desire.

> When you start a business, you must be prepared to work hard, hard, hard for four to seven years before you achieve the financial success you desire.

The Two Key Qualities

The two most important ingredients for entrepreneurship are, first, the *courage* to take great risks with your time and your money, and second, the *persistence* to endure month after month and year after year until you finally succeed.

Fully 80 percent of people who leave the security of a salaried job to start a business find that it is not the right career choice for them. They quickly become discouraged at the long hours and unending problems. They find that they are not happy working alone and being responsible for everything, including sweeping the floors and cleaning the toilets. They need the comfort, companionship, and security of working within a larger organization where they can specialize and where there are people around them to do many of the support tasks.

Your primary goal in life should be to be *happy*. You will be happy as an entrepreneur only if you really love what you are doing and are capable of putting your whole heart into building your business, year after year, with very little to show for it at the beginning. The time to decide if entrepreneurship is right for you is before you launch, not later on, after you have invested months of your life and lost thousands of your hard-earned dollars.

3. Select the Business That's Right for You

Starting a business is like getting married. There must be a high level of compatibility between the person you are and the type of business you are thinking of starting. Some people fail in one kind of business but succeed greatly in another because they were not suited to one kind of enterprise but ideally suited for something else.

Ralph Waldo Emerson once wrote, "Nothing succeeds without enthusiasm." Your ability to develop and sustain a high level of enthusiasm for what you are doing is essential to keep you going in the face of obstacles and difficulties. You will be successful producing and selling only a product or service that you really believe in and care about, something you would be happy selling to your father, mother, or best friend.

Start with Yourself

Begin with your talents, abilities, experience, knowledge, interests, and background. You will be successful only doing something that you really enjoy, something that interests you, absorbs you, and grabs your attention. When you look back over your previous activities, you will find that there have been products, services, and activities that attracted you. These can be good indicators of the kind of business you should be in today. You will always be most successful doing something or marketing something that you really *love*.

When you start a business, begin by looking for something that is an improvement on an existing product or service rather than something that is brand new. Look for something that you can bring to the market cheaper, faster, more easily, and in better quality or with additional features or benefits. Remember: an idea only needs to be 10-percent new and better to capture substantial market share.

Read everything you can find about potential businesses. Keep your eyes open for a product or service that people need but that no one is offering. Talk to your friends. Look around in your own job or field. There may be a million-dollar idea staring you in the face in the form of something that you think someone should be offering to the market in which you live and work.

Keep alert and open to new business opportunities occurring around you. Especially, listen to your *inner voice*. What sort of product or service would you really like to bring to the market and build a successful business around? This is the starting point of starting your business.

4. Identify Your Customers Clearly

The most important single question in market research and sales planning is the question, *"Who is my customer?"* Failure to answer this question with great clarity is the number-one reason why businesses fail. Because the people at the top are not clear about their customers, they pro-

> The most important single question in market research and sales planning is the question, *"Who is my customer?"*

duce a product or service for customers who do not exist or not in sufficient quantity to make the businesses successful.

Who is your customer, exactly? Describe him or her in detail. What is his or her age? What sort of education does he or she have? What is his or her income? What sort of work does he or she do and at what level? What is his or her background or experience, especially as it relates to your product or service? What are his or her interests, beliefs, values, or attitudes? Take all this information and write out a description of your *ideal customer*, the perfect customer for the product or service you are thinking of offering.

Why Does Your Customer Buy?

You then ask yourself questions about motivation. "Why does my customer buy this product? What does my potential customer consider to be value in what I sell? What benefits does he or she seek? What is the primary motivation that causes my customer to buy what I sell? What does my product or service do for my customer? What is the most important benefit that my customer enjoys from using my product or service? And above all, what does my customer have to be convinced of to buy this product or service from me rather than from someone else?"

For a new product or service business to enter the market, it must be better by a *factor of three*. It must be faster, cheaper, or easier to use. It must better is some important way or contain additional features and benefits. It must be sold more professionally, delivered more efficiently, and serviced more rapidly. In what three ways is your product or service superior to what is already available?

How Large Is the Market?

Is the market for your product or service large enough? Are there enough potential customers to make your business a success? Is your market concentrated enough? Can you reach your market with sufficient advertising, promotional, and selling activities to sell enough and make enough profit?

Whenever a company, large or small, is having problems with sales and cash flow, like many of the Internet companies today, the problems can almost always be traced back to a failure of the company to correctly identify the potential customers and then to reach those customers in sufficient quantity and get them to buy in a timely and cost effective manner.

5. Do Fast, Cheap Market Research Before Spending Money

It is easy to fall in love with a product or service idea. But before you invest your time, your money, and your life in a business venture, you should investigate it carefully to make sure that potential customers are as excited about your product or service as you are.

The payoff for careful market research will be more than ten to one in the money that you will save or earn as a result and time and that you will save.

Do your homework. Invest your time and energy rather than your money to prove that people will buy your product—before you bring it to the market.

Become an Expert

Begin by finding out every detail of the product or service. Treat it like a research product. Read trade magazines, articles, and stories on the business, industry, or occupation. Surf the Internet for every bit of information you can find.

Seek out people in the same business and ask for their opinions of the product or service. Don't be secretive. People in the same business will give you very good feedback on the viability of your idea.

Ask your bank manager for his or her opinion or advice. Bank managers see hundreds of business ideas every year. They are extremely knowledgeable about what is likely to work in the marketplace. A five-minute conversation with my bank manager some years ago saved me $200,000 in buying a business. He pointed out two or three things that I had completely overlooked because of my inexperience.

Ask your friends, your family, and your acquaintances for information, input, and ideas about your business idea.

Ask a Customer

Especially, visit prospective customers and ask if they would buy that product or service from you. Ask if they could sell the product or service to others.

Act as if you had been hired as a consultant to evaluate this potential business. Develop a suspicious attitude and accept nothing on faith. Look for what I call the "fatal flaw" in the business idea. Then, look at the business as though you were going to be in it for the next 20 years. Is this what you had in mind?

Many businesspeople will take a year or more before they finally decide which business to enter or which products or services to bring to the market. Every hour you spend in research and test-marketing will save you ten hours of hard work later on.

Be Sure That a Market Exists

Remember the story of the entrepreneur in Chapter 3 who thought he would make a killing on the toy creepy crawly spiders the bought from a Taiwanese manufacturer. He invested more than he could probably afford, buying 10,000 units for $3 each and kept what he was doing secret, with the idea he was certain to make a killing at Christmas.

He called a major department store and told the buyer he had a great toy that would sell like crazy during the Christmas season. He got his appointment and when he demonstrated his toy, the buyer loved it. In fact, he had already bought 100,000 units from the same manufacturer for $1.59 each. The market was there, but because he didn't check out whether he could sell these toys at a profit, he lost his shirt (not to mention his money).

Test the Market

Test-marketing is quite simple. First, you make a prototype or create a sample of the product or service that you can show to a potential customer. You then get accurate prices and delivery dates from your suppliers so you know exactly how much you will have to charge. With these in hand, you go straight to a buyer and ask for his or her opinion about your product or service. Ask prospective customers whether they would buy the product or service and what price they would pay for it. If you are selling to companies, call on the individual who makes the final buying decision and get his or her candid reaction to your offering.

Be sure to compare your product with other products on the market. You must always answer the question, "Why would someone buy from you instead of from someone else?"

Another way to test-market a new product or service is to take it to a trade

> You must always answer the question, "Why would someone buy from you instead of from someone else?"

show where sophisticated buyers and potential customers will tell you whether or not you have a winner.

Finally, ask your friends, your relatives, and your business associates if they would buy or use the product or service at the price that you would have to charge.

I once bought $2,000 worth of a home cleaning product that I thought everyone would want. It turned out that nobody wanted it at all and I ended up stuck with the product for years. Don't let this happen to you.

6. Approach Your Business Strategically

Stand back and look at your business from the point of view of an objective third party. Imagine hiring a professional to inspect your business and ask you some hard questions before you start. Be tough on yourself and your own ideas. This alone can give you a key advantage over your competitors. The more time you spend thinking through the answers to these hard questions, the less time it will take you to pay for your mistakes and turn your business into a profitable enterprise.

Ask the Key Questions

First, what exactly do you sell, in terms of what it does for your customer? What need of your customers does it satisfy that is currently not being satisfied by someone else's product or service?

The three major needs of customers are *better, faster,* and *cheaper.* Customers also want products and services that are easy to use and superior to what they are using currently. Business customers specifically want increased sales, lower costs, and higher net profits. Individual customers want things like success, social status, popularity, knowledge, influence, and personal power. People in general want prestige, admiration, acceptance, self-esteem, pleasure, and comfort. Which of these needs does your product satisfy?

Customers always act to improve their situations, either personal or business, in some way. In what specific ways does your product or service improve the life or work of your customers? You must be very clear and specific about this.

Determine Your Mission

A key part of strategic thinking is to know why you are doing what you are doing. What is your mission for being in business? What kind of a difference do you want to make in the lives of your customers?

Every successful business is built around a central purpose or mission—and the very best mission is always to help people to improve their lives in some way. How would you describe your mission in this respect?

What does your customer consider value? What does your customer actually buy? What is your customer seeking that he or she does not have already? The clearer you can be about the value that you are bringing to the life or work of your customer, the easier it is for you to design all of your marketing and sales activities.

Where Do You Excel?

What is your area of excellence? What is your competitive advantage? What do you do better than anyone else that your customer is willing to pay you for? Every product or service offering must have one or more areas of excellence that enable it to stand out from any other competitive offerings in the marketplace. What are yours?

Who is competing for the attention and the dollars of your customer? Who is selling something else that your customers could just as easily buy rather than buying from you? Your ability to clearly identify your competition actually determines everything you do in building your own successful business.

Identify Your Competition

Not long ago, I worked with the Caribbean Cruise Line. They do not define their competition as other cruise ships. They define their competition as anyone who is accustomed to taking a land-based vacation, anywhere in the world. Since only 5 percent of people have been on cruise ships, they aim all of their marketing and sales efforts at the 95 percent of people who have not yet taken a cruise. They have determined that their competition is any way that a person could spend money on any kind of vacation (including staying at home) that does not involve a cruise on one of their ships. Who or what is your competition for your customers' dollars?

Why does your customer buy from your competition? What benefits or advantages does your customer see in buying from your competitors rather than from you? What do you have to do to convince your customer to change from his or her current supplier of products or services similar to yours and switch to you? Your ability to convey the meaningful differentiation between what you sell and what your competitors sell is central to your success. How is your product or service different or better?

Why Should Someone Buy from You?

Your ability to list several reasons why an intelligent customer should buy your product or service in a competitive market is central to all your sales and marketing efforts. Your ability to answer the question, "Why should someone buy from me?" will largely determine your success or failure in business.

Write out several reasons why someone should buy from you. Share these reasons with other people in your family or business and ask for their opinions. Then, focus on the one or two advantages in buying from you that no other company or individual can offer. This difference then becomes the focal point of all of your promotional efforts. Your ability to convey these ideas into the hearts and minds of your customers will largely determine how much you sell and how fast you grow.

7. Develop a Complete Business Plan Before Starting

This is one of the most difficult and yet one of the most important processes if you want to start and build a successful business. Many successful entrepreneurs take weeks and even months developing their business plans before they launch their enterprises. Fortunately, you can get software (Business Plan Pro) that will help you put a business plan together far more easily than by hand. And you must do it *yourself*. You cannot get someone else to develop a business plan for you. This would be the same as getting someone else to select a husband or wife for you without involving you.

> The major benefit of a business plan is that it forces you to think through every element of the business in advance.

The major benefit of a business plan is that it forces you to think through every element of the business in advance. A business plan is really quite simple. It requires that you project exactly how much of what product or service you are going to sell each month and each year for the next year to 18 months. You then calculate the total cost of producing and delivering these products or services. You determine everything you will need—real estate, facilities, equipment, advertising, staff, furniture, and so forth—in order to bring these products or services to the market. You calculate how much money you will need and where you will get that money. Finally, you project how much profit you are going to make and when you are going to make it.

Be Realistic About Your Business

Here are two rules that could save your business life. First, everything costs twice as much as you think it will. Second, everything takes three times as long as you estimate.

This means that if your budget for an activity is $10,000, it will end up costing you $20,000 or more. If you expect to break even in three months, you will probably not break even before nine months, maybe even later. And one final point: remember that Murphy's Law was developed by an entrepreneur—*"Whatever can go wrong will go wrong."* And the first corollary of Murphy's Law is *"Of all the things that can go wrong, the worst possible thing will go wrong at the worst possible time and cost the very most money."*

> Two rules of business life: First, everything costs twice as much as you think it will. Second, everything takes three times as long as you estimate.

Once you have designed and printed your business plan, show it to as many experienced people as possible and invite their feedback. Be prepared to revise your business plan when you get new information. Once it is complete, your business plan becomes the blueprint for building your business, just as you would develop a final blueprint for constructing your house. You then use your business plan as your guide in steering your business through the turbulent seas ahead.

8. Do Everything Possible to Ensure Business Success

There are certain requirements, based on the study of tens of thousands of successful businesses, that you can fulfill to ensure that your business is successful. The first requirement is that your product or service is *well suited* to the wants and needs of the current market. This is perhaps the most important success principle of all.

The second is that you develop a complete *business plan* before you start operations. You take the time to think things through before investing your money.

The third requirement is that you do a complete *market analysis* before starting your advertising and sales promotion activities.

Fourth, you implement tight financial controls, good budgeting practices, and accurate bookkeeping and accounting and you practice frugality in every business activity. Run a tight ship. Squeeze every dollar. Cash is to the life of the business as oxygen is to the brain. Guard it carefully.

The fifth requirement for business success is that the key people have a high degree of competence, capability, and integrity. In addition, there should be good internal efficiency, good time management, and clear job descriptions. All members of the team should know what they are expected to do and when they are expected to do it.

Finally, perhaps the most important requirement for business success is that there be a strong momentum in the *sales department* and a total focus on marketing the product or service. Concern for the customer must be a top priority at all times. Everyone in the company thinks about sales and top-line revenues, all day, every day until the company is well into the black.

9. Avoid the Mistakes That Lead to Business Failure

Major accounting and consulting firms have done autopsies on thousands of businesses that failed. These studies conclude that most business failures have certain things in common, every one of which you should consciously avoid, every single day.

The first reason for business failure is *lack of direction*. This is demonstrated as a failure to establish specific goals for each part of the business. In addition, a company lacks direction when it does not have a complete business plan.

The second reason for failure is *impatience*—trying to accomplish too much too soon. This is often demonstrated by spending too much on advertising at the beginning rather than building up a customer base gradually. Remember: everything costs twice as much and takes three times as long as your best guess.

The third reason for failure is *greed*, trying to charge too much, get rich quick, or sell a lot of products or services without building a market reputation. It is always better to go for a reasonable profit at the beginning and raise your prices as demand increases.

The fourth reason for failure is *poor cost control*. This is demonstrated by over-spending, especially at the beginning. Remember: cash is everything. Conserve cash at all costs. When the cash is gone, the company is gone as well.

A fifth reason for failure is *poor quality* of the product or service. This makes it difficult to sell initially and almost impossible to sell later. Poor quality even makes it difficult to get paid for what you have sold.

The sixth major reason for failure is *insufficient working capital*. The business runs out of money because it does not budget ahead far enough. This is why a good business plan is so important.

The seventh major reason for failure is *insufficient sales* and a loss of momentum in the sales department. People get so busy operating the business that they forget that without sales there is no business. It is vital that you focus on selling and make all other business activities secondary to that.

10. Remember the Purpose of the Business

What is the purpose of a business? Most people answer that the purpose of a business is to "make a profit." However, that is not quite correct. The real purpose of a business is to create and keep a customer. Making a profit is the result of creating and keeping a customer in a cost-effective way.

> The real purpose of a business is to create and keep a customer. Making a profit is the result of creating and keeping a customer in a cost-effective way.

Here are the key questions for strategy for your business.

First, what business are you *really* in? Define your business in terms of what your product or service does to improve the life or work of your customers.

Second, what is your *mission*? What is your *vision* for your business? What do you really want to achieve for your customers with your product or service? Describe a totally satisfied customer.

Third, if your business were *ideal* in every way, what would it look like? How would people talk about your business? What level of sales would you have? What level of profits? How fast would you be growing each month? Each year? What kind of products and services would you offer? What kind of people would you have working for you? What kind of customers would you be serving?

The more clearly you think through and answer these questions, the better the decisions you will make and the more successful your business will be, both in the short term and in the long term.

11. Focus on the Five Main P's of Marketing

There are five P's to successful marketing. Whenever you have problems in sales, it is because one of these five P's is wrong in some way. Often, one change in one P can improve your sales and profitability dramatically.

The first P stands for *product*. What exactly is the product or service that you are offering and is it appropriate and desirable for the current market? If people are not buying it in sufficient quantity, find out if what you are offering is what they are interested in buying.

The second P stands for *price*. How much are you asking for your product or service and is this an appropriate price? Is it competitive in today's market? Is it enough to justify bringing the product or service to the market in the first place? Can you make a profit at that price? Should you lower your price or charge differently for what you sell?

The third P is *place*. This is where you sell your product or service. Sometimes, one location or geographical area can be vastly better than another in enabling you to sell large quantities of what you offer. Some companies have transformed their industries by moving from direct sales forces who sell in the home or office to distributor sales forces who sell through retail channels. Could there be a better place for you to offer your product or service?

The fourth P stands for *promotion*. How do you advertise and market your product? Is your advertising effective? Are you reaching a sufficient number of prospective customers in a cost-effective way? Sometimes, a small change in the way you promote your product or service can lead to an enormous change in your sales results.

The final P stands for *positioning*. This is often the most important part of sales and marketing. Your positioning is how your customers think and feel about your product or service.

What kind of a *reputation* do you have? How do people think about and talk about your product? What unique selling propositions of your product or service stand out in your customers' minds as the result of your sales and marketing efforts? What impression does your product or service make in the minds of the people to whom you want to sell it?

You must be absolutely crystal clear about where you are with all five P's — *product, price, place, promotion,* and *positioning.* If your sales are not high enough, go back and review these factors one by one and make whatever changes are necessary. This is essential to building a successful, profitable business.

12. Focus Single-Mindedly on Sales

In starting and building your business, sales are more important than anything else. Sales are the primary source of cash flow, which is critical for the survival of the enterprise. Every successful business has high and predictable levels of sales. Every unsuccessful business has problems in sales.

Most successful businesses are started by a person who is very good at selling the product or service. And the key to selling the product or service is to develop a professional sales presentation, both written and in person, and then to make this presentation to as many people as possible, every single day.

Play the Numbers

The Law of Probabilities predicts sales success. This law says that the more people you tell about your product or service, the more of your product or service you will sell. If you want to increase your sales, you must increase your frequency of customer contact. You must continually prospect, present, and follow up, every single day.

You must use every possible means of *contacting* more and more prospective customers. You must use every form of advertising, including telemarketing. You must get out face to face with customers, tell them why they will be better off using your product or service, and ask them to make a buying decision. Every successful company in the world today has one or more excellent salespeople who are selling the product or service, all day long. Every company in trouble has problems in the sales department.

As the entrepreneur and company owner, you must focus single-mindedly on sales and delegate every other activity to someone else. Make a decision today to become an absolute expert in professional selling. Read every book, listen to every audio program, and attend every course until you have far too many sales for your company to be able to handle. Until your company is overwhelmed by sales, your entire focus should be on the sales function.

13. Advertise Your Product or Service Continually

Doing business without advertising is like winking at a woman in the dark: only you know what you are doing. You have to advertise and promote all the time. Nonetheless, you must do it prudently.

When you start off, the very best sales promotion is one on one, with perhaps letters, faxes, or e-mails in advance, followed by telephone calls and personal face-to-face visits with prospective customers. It is amazing how many small businesspeople try to replace the personal act of selling with the impersonal act of general advertising. Don't make this mistake.

There are three keys to successful advertising. They are: *test, test, test!* Be prepared to try several different advertisements, in several different media, until you find something that really works.

Creative Advertising Sells

Here is the rule: "Creative advertising sells." If your advertising is good, it will sell immediately. You will get immediate responses. If you do not get immediate sales, stop doing that particular type of advertising—immediately. You are wasting your money and actually hurting your business.

Your advertising should offer *one specific benefit* that the customer will enjoy by calling you, by coming into your place of business, or by using your product or service. A seven-year-old child should be able to look at your advertisement and explain to another seven-year-old exactly what you are offering and why it is attractive to a prospective customer. If your advertising does not pass the "seven-year-old test," revise it and rewrite it until it does.

Set aside a specific percentage of your sales revenue for advertising and continue to experiment for the rest of your business life. Some advertising works well. Some advertising does not work at all.

> Set aside a specific percentage of your sales revenue for advertising and continue to experiment for the rest of your business life.

Some offers work well and some offers have no effect. Fully 50 percent of advertising dollars are wasted—but no one knows for sure which ones they are. Test, test, test, and then test again until you find an advertising campaign that really pays off.

14. Use the Internet to Boost Your Sales

Within a few years, fully half of the sales in America are going to be either made on the Internet or facilitated by the Internet. The sales that are not done directly via the Internet will be preceded by market research on the Internet before customers call you or visit your place of business.

The good news is that you can start a Web site quickly and inexpensively. Companies like Yahoo and Microsoft will help you build a storefront and then operate it for you for a few dollars per month. As your company grows, you can hire a larger firm that will build a more comprehensive Web site.

But whatever you do, register your business name as a domain name as quickly as possible. Then, set up a Web site with information about your products and services, very much like an electronic brochure. Put your URL (Web address) on all of your material. Have an e-mail address on your Web site so customers can get in touch with you and ask you questions. Keep your Web site updated regularly. Send e-mail messages to your customers informing them of product or service specials.

If you are not comfortable with computers and the Internet, run, don't walk to your nearest computer store and get yourself outfitted immediately. Fortunately, most of the bugs have been removed from the computer and the technology of the Internet. It is now possible for children to set up Web sites and surf the world of information, products, and services. This can be one of the smartest things you do in starting and building a successful business.

15. Practice the Corridor Principle

In a 13-year study at Babson College, researchers conducted follow-up interviews with graduates of the entrepreneurship program to find out why some had started businesses after graduation and succeeded and some had done nothing with their education. In almost every case, they found that the successful entrepreneurs had only *one quality* that made them differ-ent from the others: they had launched their businesses with no guarantee of success.

> The successful entrepreneurs had only *one quality* that made them different from the others: they had launched their businesses with no guarantee of success.

The failures, on the other hand, were still waiting for every-thing to be just right before they started their businesses. And, of course, things will never be just right. If you wait for things to be just right, you will wait forever.

As the successful entrepreneurs launched their new businesses, they began moving along what they called a "corridor." As they moved down the corridor of business life, doors opened on either side of them that led them to new possibilities and new opportunities. What they discovered was that, if they had not been moving forward toward their business goals, they would not have seen the doors that were opening up along the "corridor." And in most cases, their business successes came in fields apart from where they had started and with products or services that were completely different from the ones they had tried at the start.

Orison Swett Marden, the founder of *Success Magazine* in 1895, once said that the two keys to business success are "get-to-it-iveness" and "stick-to-it-iveness." Do your homework. Make your plans and then *launch* in the direction of your business goals. Everything else will take care of itself. If you wait until success is ensured before you start, you will end up waiting forever.

16. Get the Money You Need

When you start a business, you will need lots and lots of money. You will never have enough. This is why you must carefully guard your cash at all times. If you run out of cash, your business can die overnight.

Here are some facts about entrepreneurship and money. First, 99 percent of new businesses are started with what is called "love money." This is your own money, from your savings and your personal borrowings. It is money from people who love you and who are willing to take a chance on you.

Banks do not lend money to start-ups. Banks are in the business of making good loans that are sure to be paid back, with interest. A bank considering a loan request will usually require that the applicant prove that he or she has five dollars to back up every dollar of the loan. In addition, the bank will want personal guarantees from the applicant, his or her spouse, and any other acquaintance with assets.

Once your business gets going and you have positive cash flow, you can increase your chances of borrowing money from your bank by going in with a complete business plan, a personal financial statement, and next year's budget projections to show your banker that you know what you are doing.

Ask for a specific amount of money or line of credit and give the banker a specific date or schedule by which you will repay the money.

What Banks Require to Loan Money

Banks look for five essentials, the 5 C's, before approving a loan. The first C is your *character*, which includes your background and your reputation in the community. The second C is your *capacity*, your ability to repay the loan from the level of sales and profits in your business. The third C bankers look for is *collateral*, the security you can provide that they can seize in case you do not repay the loan. The fourth C is *capital*, the amount of your own money that you have invested or that you are prepared to invest along with their money. And the fifth C that they look for is *credit*, the status of your credit to date going back over your entire life.

You can often borrow from friends, relatives, and even private investors who will take a share of your company and a share of your profits in exchange for investing in your business. But even here, you should have a complete business plan to show them.

The very best policy for starting and building a successful business is to start small, sell vigorously, and grow by reinvesting the profits in the business. This is called "bootstrapping," where you grow more slowly but your growth is built on a foundation of hard work and solid cash flow. When you bootstrap, you seem to get far smarter, far faster than you would if you started off with too much money.

However you finance your business, you must always be careful about how much money you have and how much you need. Never allow yourself to run out of cash.

17. Make Use of Technology

We are living in the age of technology. You can use technology in many ways to serve your customers better, faster, cheaper, and easier. You can use technology to communicate quickly with customers and prospects. You can use technology to send out information quickly and do fast, cheap market research. You can use technology to sell more and more of your products, over a wider and wider market, at a lower and lower price.

All of technology develops around the concept of saving time getting specific results, especially business results. And since your time is your most valuable resource, you should use every single type of technology—including pagers, cell phones, fax machines, the Internet, and portable equipment—to do your job and take care of your customers faster and better than your competitors. By using technology properly, you can dramatically reduce the number of staff you require to run your business efficiently and well. Ask questions, read magazines, get advice, and be open to the technological advances around you that can help you to build a successful, profitable business.

> By using technology properly, you can dramatically reduce the number of staff you require to run your business efficiently and well.

And always remember that if it works, it is already obsolete. Fully 80 percent of the products and services you will be using in your business in five years will be new and different from today. Many of them have not yet been invented.

18. Make Every Minute Pay

Your time is your most precious resource. It is all you really have to sell. Use the 80/20 rule on everything in your business: 20 percent of your activities will account for 80 percent of your results. Discipline yourself to always be working on the top 20 percent that make all the difference to your success.

Never fall into the temptation to clear up small things first. As an independent entrepreneur, the most important thing you do is to select your most important task and then dedicate yourself to doing just that one thing until it is complete.

Doubling Your Productivity

Here is a simple five-step technique that you can use to double and triple your overall productivity, performance, and output. First, start every day with a list of activities, made out the night before. Second, organize the list by priorities. Put an A, B, or C next to each item before you begin. Your "A" items are the most important of all, the items for which there can be substantial *consequences* if you do them or don't do them. Your "B" items are items you *should* do but that are not as important as your "A" items. Your "C" items are items that would be *nice* for you to do, but it doesn't really matter if you do them or not.

Here is the rule. Never do a "B" item when there is an "A" item you have not done. If you have several "A" items, set priorities by listing them as A-1, A-2, A-3, and so on. This is where you get maximum payoff from your time.

The third key to time management is for you to begin on your A-1 task first thing in the morning and stay with it until it is complete. Work without diversion or distraction. Discipline yourself to focus and concentrate on that one item, even if it takes you all day long. This is the very highest and best use of your time.

Step four in time management is to keep focused by asking yourself *three key questions*, every hour of every day. Question number one is *"What are my highest-value activities?"* Ask your co-workers and staff this question as well. Whatever the answer is to that question, that is what you should probably be doing at the moment.

The second question you can ask yourself is *"What can I, and only I do, that if I do it well, will make a real difference?"* There is only one answer to that question at any given time—and that is what you should be working on.

The third question, perhaps the best of all, is *"What is the most valuable use of my time right now?"* Ask this question over and over again and make sure that, whatever your answer, it is what you are working on most of the time.

The fifth key to great time management is to develop a *sense of urgency*, a bias for action. Move fast on opportunities and responsibilities. Do it now! Develop a reputation for doing the job quickly and well. This alone can guarantee you success in your business.

19. Dedicate Yourself to Lifelong Learning

Continuous learning is the minimum requirement for success in your field. Lifelong learning is the key to the 21st century. All leaders are *learners*. For you to succeed greatly in a competitive field, you must stay ahead of your competitors by adding to your knowledge and skills continually.

The highest-paid businesspeople in America read two to three hours each day in their field. If you read only one hour per day in your field, that will translate into about one book per week, 50 books per year. By reading one, two, or three hours per day in your field, you will not only stay current, but also become one of the smartest and highest-paid people in your business.

Listen to audio programs in your car. The average car owner sits in his or her car 500 to 1000 hours each year. This is equal to 12 to 24 40-hour weeks behind the wheel. A good audio program contains the best ideas of 30-50 books. You can get the equivalent of attending a university full time by listening to educational audio programs as you drive around.

Finally, take every seminar and course that you can. Many people have become wealthy in business as the result of a single book, a single audio program, or a single seminar.

Take time every day to upgrade your knowledge and skills. As Pat Riley, the basketball coach, said, "If you're not getting better, you're getting worse." Your job is to get better every single day.

20. Hire Slow and Fire Fast

Fully 95 percent of your success will be determined by the people you hire to work for you. In the early stages of your business, your turnover will be very high, as much as 200 percent each year. This is to be expected. The rule in this area is simple: "Hire slow and fire fast."

In fact, the very best time to fire a person is usu-

> Fully 95 percent of your success will be determined by the people you hire to work for you.

ally the first time it occurs to you. Always ask yourself, "If I had not hired this person, knowing what I now know, would I hire him or her back again today?" If the answer is no, then your only question is "How do I get rid of him and how fast?"

Look for people with good attitudes and pleasant personalities. Look for people who are willing to work hard. Look for people that you like and enjoy. Look for people who believe in what you are doing and who can become committed to your work. And if you make a hiring mistake, let the person go as quickly as possible.

One of the major reasons for small business failure is the inability to let go of an incompetent person for fear of hurting his or her feelings. Don't let this happen to you.

21. Practice the Seven Secrets of Success

There are seven key activities you can practice to greatly increase your chances of great success in business and in life:

- Decide exactly what you want, write it down, and work on it every day. Review your goals each morning and each evening.

- Determine the price you will have to pay to achieve your goals and then resolve to pay that price. Get started immediately.

- Accept 100-percent responsibility for your life and everything that you are or ever will be. Say over and over to yourself, *"If it's to be, it's up to me!"*

- Make a total commitment to your success. Burn your bridges. Never think of turning back. Keep reminding yourself, *"Failure is not an option."*

- Be willing to work hard, hard, hard. Be willing to go the extra mile and always do more than you are paid for. This is the key to success in your business.

- Use your time well, every minute, every hour, and every day. Your time is all you have to sell. Keep focused on your highest-value activities.

- Back your plans with determination and persistence. Resolve in advance that you will *never give up*. Persistence is perhaps the most important quality you can develop to guarantee your eventual success.

Pulling It All Together

Let me summarize with these points. There are thousands of books on small business success. You can even take a five- or six-year MBA program on the subject requiring thousands of hours of study. But the 21 great ideas in this chapter run through every single book, magazine, and course on entrepreneurship you will ever read, attend, or hear about.

The most important part of this book is what you decide to do as a result. All successful people and entrepreneurs are *action-oriented.* They are constantly in motion. They are busy all the time. To become action-oriented, you must develop a sense of urgency. It is what you do *now* that determines your future.

Summary

This is the greatest time in all of human history to be alive. There have never been more opportunities for more people to make more money and to achieve financial independence than now.

There is nothing in the world that can stop you from becoming a millionaire or even a multimillionaire in your business, other than yourself. When you learn and do what other successful people have done, as we have taught in this book, you will soon get the results that other successful people get. There are no limits!

Action Exercises

1. Determine what business you are really in. What does your product or service achieve, avoid, or preserve for your customer?

2. Identify your competitive advantage. Why should someone buy from you rather than from your competitor?

3. Focus on sales every day. What could you do to increase the quantity and quality of your sales today?

4. Who is your ideal customer? Where is he or she and why does he or she buy from you or from your competitor?

5. Look before you leap: develop a complete business plan before you start and then upgrade it every year.

6. Use your time well; always focus on the most valuable use of your time.

7. What one activity could have the greatest positive impact on your business right now? Whatever it is, start immediately on that task and stay at it until it is 100-percent complete.

INDEX

Index

Timing principle, 171–173
Trade shows, 57, 221
TRAF system, 197–198
Training systems, 47
Traveling, product/services ideas from,
58–59
Trends, 59–60, 65
Trust
establishing in sales process, 92,
116–117
importance to success, 21
Turnaround specialists, 37–38
20/10 exercise, 34

U
Ultimate question, 100–102
Uncertainty principle, 13–14
Unique selling proposition, 39, 81,
121
Unlimited possibilities principle,
168–169
Urgency, 203, 213, 238, 241

V
Value added, 29
Value of tasks, 195

Values, 16, 21–22
Variable costs, 137–138, 152
Variable pricing, 145–147
Vision, 16
Volume discounts, 146

W
Walkaway price, 148
Walk-away principle, 182–183
Walkman players, 59
Wal-Mart, 54, 80, 141
Web sites, 232–233
Winning edge in sales, 111–115
Win/win principle in negotiation,
166–168
Women, discussing product/service
ideas with, 64
Working capital, 227
Worktime, increasing, 204
Writing goals, 213, 214

X
Xerox, 147

Z
Zero-based thinking, 184